KT-442-250

You'll find tips, advice on troubleshooting and practical activities to help you develop your skills, complete with stories from the authors' own experience. Chapters 8 and 9 contain useful guidance on how to handle unexpected responses when coaching. The last chapter includes a list of resources to take your journey of discovery further.

Crucially, the book reminds us that a manager as coach is there to facilitate others to accomplish things in their own way; as opposed to the traditional sense of a manager as the leader, defining others' goals, specifying their activity and making them accountable.

A very welcome addition to the library of self-help books for managers.

Gillian Phillips, Director of Editorial Legal Services,
Guardian News & Media Limited

The Five-Minute Coach sets out a technique that focuses on desired outcomes and that has relevance well beyond individual coaching. Lynne and Mariette show how a simple approach, that is fully independent of the coach's personal opinions or knowledge, can enable insights and solutions to emerge. Presented in a refreshingly clear and easily digestible format, the book contains a wealth of practical tips and case studies that guide the reader through. A useful addition to the armoury of any coach – from the manager of a team of staff to the parent of teenagers.

Marian Ridley, Joint Director of Strategy,
Guy's & St Thomas' NHS Foundation Trust

I found *The Five Minute Coach* an original, simple, yet highly effective approach to achieving change at an individual level or within a group, and in diverse situations. It shows how some very small changes in the coach's language can effect a big change; it makes the power of coaching accessible to all, with clear outcome and action focussed processes and questions.

Michèle Moore, Head of People Development, Elior UK

Once you have got your head around the concept of Clean Language *The Five-Minute Coach* is an essential approach for busy managers and internal coaches who need to make a difference fast. With a little preparation and background reading, the approach can be deployed quickly and effectively in many operational management situations. I particularly liked the way the technique focused on getting the individual to really focus on their own interference and how to unblock it without the coach getting in the way.

The Five-Minute Coach book is full of helpful advice and guidance. I particularly liked the use of case studies, exercises and simple templates to bring Five-Minute coaching to life. As a professional coach, it will certainly be a technique I'll be using personally and sharing with coaching and business colleagues alike.

Mike Corker, Global Lead for Talent and Learning & Development, Capgemini Infrastructure Services

Clean Language is a greatly under-rated technique for coaches and here it's explained in a really easy and helpful way.

Anyone who is looking for an easy to remember, structured approach to improving outcomes in their work life, or as a coach, should definitely have this book on their shelf/e-reader.

Sean Finnan, General Manager, IBM Global Technology Services

The temptation to just do it yourself rather than help a team member to learn how to do something is very real for busy managers. *The Five-Minute Coach* leaves you with no excuse for doing that. It takes the reader through a helpfully structured approach and offers both effective tools and really useful tips along the way.

Reading this book made me think hard about the way I manage my own staff and reappraise my approach. Its clarity about how to make a real difference through effective coaching makes it a valuable addition to any manager's briefcase.

Sir Steve Bullock, Executive Mayor, London Borough of Lewisham

Praise for *The Five Minute Coach*

The Five-Minute Coach is an excellent introduction to the principles and use of Clean Language. I have been coaching for many years and have known a little about Clean Language, but not enough to feel confident to use it. This book has been immediately useful to me because Chapter 1 gets stuck straight away into a step by step 'how to' guide, which is perfect for a Clean Language beginner like me. Even better than this, it really does only take 5 minutes to prepare to use the process and then 5 minutes to actually 'do the coaching'. It's not often that you can read a book and get started on the techniques when you're only half way through Chapter 1, but this is refreshingly the case with *The Five-Minute Coach*. The rest of the book expands upon the coaching skills and personal attributes of the coach that will add depth and power to the technique itself, with stories and case studies along the way to support the authors' findings and thoughts. I can't wait to receive my copy of this book as I will definitely be recommending it to all those I work with to develop and enhance their coaching skills.

Clare Smale, Coach and Trainer, Inspired2learn

Quite simply the best coaching book I've ever read.

In spite of being extremely busy with some major projects at present, I read it from cover to cover. It gives a simple exposition of the process, explaining ideas and techniques that are easy to apply and work extremely well.

I find myself using the ideas set out in this book, not only with the people in my team, but also with colleagues across the company (and with my kids at home, too). I will be recommending this book to both friends and colleagues.

Clive Bach, Assistant Vice President, Midrange manager for Apps dev and test, Bank of America Merrill Lynch

A well written and structured book. I started off thinking 'this isn't for me' because I couldn't imagine myself a) carrying out many formal coaching sessions and b) being able use a 'clean' approach as the

BROMLEY COLLEGE LIBRARY

B58548

WITHDRAWN

temptation is to jump in with advice and 'words of wisdom'! But I have to say, I found much in the book to be extremely useful, and I can see plenty of situations in both my business and private life where applying the approaches set out in this book in an informal way could yield much better results than more traditional methods.

I particularly like all the 'Five-Minute conversations' which give some great examples of how the framework can be used in other situations.

It's a great piece of work and I'll certainly be obtaining a few copies once published to share with some of my colleagues.

David Sleath, Chief Executive, SEGRO

This book should be on every busy manager's desk. It introduces us to a technique of coaching that's tailored for busy people who need to get results swiftly. Coaching is fundamentally a non-directive technique empowering people to make their own choices. Many managers find coaching to be an effective way of managing staff but can be put off from using it because it can take too long. With this helpful book, that problem is solved. Now managers can learn a quick and easy procedure to help them support their staff, solve problems, achieve outcomes and stimulate creativity. And you get the best of all worlds - not just a happy workforce but a more productive one.

The Five-Minute Coach is based around two central tenets – delegating, so that problems end up with their rightful owners, and revolutionising thinking, so that a manager focuses on outcomes rather than the problem. Five core principles underlie *The Five-Minute Coach*: stick with the process; the coachee has all the answers; ownership is with the coachee; the manager drives the coaching; and the manager creates and manages the setting.

The chapters in the book are helpfully organised, using a series of structured questions. Chapters 1 and 2 describe the Five-Minute Coach approach and what you need to do to get started. Chapters 3–7, the key chapters, lead you through the five stages of the process. To learn the coaching approach you'll need to read them in order – at least initially.

Although coaching is not an approach I currently use, reading *The Five-Minute Coach* demonstrates clearly how this style of supporting and developing people results in positive change.

Lynne and Mariette's writing quickly establishes the use of Clean Language and clear structures in an easy to follow style. In fact, I am already reflecting on the questions they use as I participate in meetings at work, whether they are with children, parents or colleagues. A refreshing and empowering read, I hope to find someone who would coach me using *The Five-Minute Coach*.

Zoe Humm, Deputy Head, Curlew Class Teacher,
Dulwich College Kindergarten & Infants School

A very clear, easy-to-read book - both in terms of language and layout - and with a good balance between the theoretical and the practical. The examples, tips and troubleshooting really work to make it user-friendly - so a big 'thumbs up' from me!

Lisa Burnand, City Professional

I found it easy to read and the book has a good structure. It leads a person through the topic very logically and with high quality and real life examples. I genuinely believe that this book has the potential to become a "must read" for leaders at all levels, across all sectors. The way the topic is handled has really made me relook at the way I coach members of my team and it reinforced lots of lessons I had already experienced, but had forgotten or given less priority to.

Having had the experience and benefit of being coached by one of the authors, and now having read the book, this is exactly how she does it and it really does work. The changes I managed to implement post coaching in this style underline the effectiveness of it. It will be out on our suggested reading list for our leaders within Hand Picked Hotels.

Douglas Waddell, Operations Director,
Hand Picked Hotels Limited

The Five-Minute **Coach**

Improve performance - rapidly

Lynne Cooper and Mariette Castellino

The Five-Minute Coach

Improve performance - rapidly

Coaching others to high performance -
in as little as five minutes

Crown House Publishing Limited
www.crownhouse.co.uk
www.crownhousepublishing.com

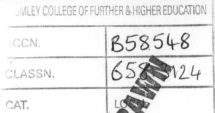

BMLEY COLLEGE OF FURTHER & HIGHER EDUCATION

CCN.	B58548
CLASSN.	658 124
CAT.	LO

WITHDRAWN

First published by

Crown House Publishing Ltd
Crown Buildings, Bancyfelin, Carmarthen,
Wales, SA33 5ND, UK
www.crownhouse.co.uk

and

Crown House Publishing Company LLC
6 Trowbridge Drive, Suite 5, Bethel, CT 06801, USA
www.crownhousepublishing.com

© Lynne Cooper and Mariette Castellino 2012

The right of Lynne Cooper and Mariette Castellino to be identified as the
authors of this work has been asserted by them in accordance with the
Copyright, Designs and Patents Act 1988.

All rights reserved. Except as permitted under current legislation no part of this work may
be photocopied (except 203), stored in a retrieval system, published, performed in public,
adapted, broadcast, transmitted, recorded or reproduced in any form or by any means, without the prior permission of the copyright owners. Enquiries should be addressed to Crown
House Publishing Limited.

The Association for Coaching's Code of Ethics and Good Coaching Practice reproduced in
Appendix III appears with their permission.

British Library Cataloguing-in-Publication Data
A catalogue entry for this book is available
from the British Library.

Print ISBN 978-184590800-3
Mobi ISBN 978-184590805-8
ePub ISBN 978-184590806-5
LCCN 2011940612

Printed and bound in the UK by
Bell & Bain Ltd, Glasgow

Crown House Publising has no responsibility for the persistence or accuracy of URLs for
external or third-party websites referred to in this publication, and does not guarantee that
any content on such websites is, or will remain, accurate or appropriate.

Foreword

David Grove – the originator of Clean Language – would have liked the Five-Minute Coach. It is true to his 'clean' philosophy and his commitment for change to originate within the individual.

When David turned his extraordinary mind to applying clean to coaching he inevitably came up with a novel approach. He recognised that the coachee's problem was often reinforced by their straight-line thinking. He therefore devised approaches which facilitated the coachee to meander through the space between where they were and where they wanted to be. Rather than going straight for what they wanted, sometimes it was preferable to first step backwards, sideways, upwards or downwards in order to see things from a different perspective and move forward from a different place.

David's great contribution was to devise processes that enabled people to discover how to do this entirely from within their own resources. This requires an extraordinary respect for the integrity of the coachee's information. Clean Language is so called because it actively keeps the coach from being tempted to help, rescue, solve, reframe or by some other means to do it for the coachee. Instead changes emerge. They occur spontaneously within the coachee's mind and body without them having to try to make anything happen – often to their great surprise.

Lynne Cooper and Mariette Castellino have taken ten Clean Language questions and artfully moulded them into the Five-Minute Coach, an easily learnable procedure that can be used to solve problems, achieve outcomes or stimulate creativity. It does not require the coach to be clever, wise, unconditionally loving or to be in control. Rather it is more like a midwife who supports the coachee to birth new ideas, new perspectives and new ways of being in the world.

The Five-Minute Coach is a very clearly written 'how to' book. Lynne's and Mariette's extensive experience as facilitators of individuals and groups underpins the explanations, examples and exercises. We strongly recommend you use this book to learn the method exactly as Lynne and Mariette have so carefully described. Then we advise you to use it over and over. By adhering to the procedure you will free yourself from having to make many decisions, especially those best left to the coachee. Then you can be more present to notice the subtle cues that enable expert coaches to work so successfully with the rhythm and uniqueness of each individual.

Lynne and Mariette are exemplary exponents of their craft and there is much to learn from them. Whether you make the Five-Minute Coach your coaching method of choice or you use it as an add-on to your existing way of coaching, you will be astounded by the results. And you'll make even more of a contribution if you integrate clean questions into your everyday conversations so that asking them becomes a natural way of supporting people to trust their own counsel. It is only then that you will discover the true value of this book.

Penny Tompkins and James Lawley
Waxahachie, Texas
1 January 2012

Acknowledgements

This book, and the Five-Minute Coach, would not have been possible without three very special people. Firstly, we are indebted to the genius of the late David Grove. His creativity, tenacity and generosity in sharing his fabulous new discoveries with others have made a significant contribution to the field of personal change.

Secondly, we remain eternally grateful to the brilliant James Lawley and Penny Tompkins. They spent many years studying David's work, developing it further, writing about it and training others to use it. Their unstinting support over more than a decade, through training, encouraging and guiding our use of Clean Language in organisations, has been priceless. We are eternally grateful.

Thanks are due to the many people in the Clean Community with whom we have worked closely over the years. In particular, we'd like to thank Caitlin Walker who whetted our appetite and mentored us through the early years, and Wendy Sullivan for her continued support and contribution to expanding the field. We are also indebted to our many, varied and wonderful clients – individuals and organisations – who have been ready and willing to work with something new and very different. Their continuing feedback has helped us to hone the Five-Minute Coach framework over many years, and their willingness to share their success stories with you is something we very much appreciate.

We are very grateful to those who put time and effort into testing this most up-to-date version of the Five-Minute Coach framework, reading the first drafts of this book and providing invaluable input. Particular thanks go to Marianne Lawrence, Steve Martin, Karen Naylor, Clive Sax, Shirley Spong, Beck Wheeler and Clive Willis. Penny and James also invested a significant amount of time offering detailed and constructive feedback. The book is much enhanced thanks to all these contributions.

We appreciate the support of all at Crown House Publishing in helping to make this book possible, including Caroline Lenton, Rosalie Williams, Beverley Randell and Tom Fitton, and the hard working team behind the scenes.

We would like to thank Glen Savage, Tim Spencer and Chelsey for their unflagging support and for keeping us fed and watered, and our friends and family who have waited patiently for our attention from the sidelines through the long hours of creating and writing this book.

Finally thanks go to each other, for having the patience, insights and fortitude to successfully complete the writing of this book together, whilst still remaining good colleagues and great friends.

Contents

A True Story

Richard works in IT at a large hospital. He introduced a new system to automate the labelling of blood samples. This works in tandem with the computerised patient record system, meaning blood tests can all be ordered electronically. A revolutionary new approach, the system is designed to increase efficiency through time-saving and reduction in transcription errors.

A few weeks after implementation, Richard had a visitor to his office. Dav works in Pathology and wanted to get a problem solved.

Dav: There's a problem with the labels from a number of wards. The barcodes are only half printing so we can't read them in the lab. It needs fixing.

Richard: OK, that sounds like a printer problem. Why don't you just speak with the wards in question and ask them to log a request with the IT service desk to have their printers realigned?

A week or so passed, and Richard had another visitor, Mindy, who also works in Pathology.

Mindy: We've still got a problem with these labels. Is anyone going to fix it?

Richard: Really? So, have you spoken with the affected wards and asked them to log a service request for the printers?

Mindy: No. It's not our problem. It's all down to this new system.

Richard: Well, I can't fix printers. The route is to ask the wards to get help to solve the problem.

Another ten days later and the Head of Pathology arrived in Richard's office.

Patrick: Richard, when are these labelling problems going to be sorted out? It's causing my team no end of problems trying to get the data sorted.

Richard: As I have already told Dav and Mindy, the problem is with some of the label printers. All they need to do is call the wards and ask them to request IT service to go and fix ...

Richard didn't have the chance to finish his sentence. Patrick was very irritated and cut across him.

Patrick: It's this new system. It's just not good enough. Can't have been properly tested, we need better service than this – it's not *our* problem.

At this point Richard groaned. No one was going to take ownership of this so he went off on a voyage of discovery himself. First to the laboratory to find one of the offending labels, then to the ward it had come from. There he spoke to a nurse.

Richard: These labels are printing incorrectly as I'm sure you can see. I wonder if you could call in IT service to get it fixed?

Nurse: It's not our printer. It was just stuck here with these labels. We weren't trained in what to do. It's not our problem.

At this point a frustrated Richard went to the IT service manager and explained that some of the blood test label printers around the hospital needed resetting.

Julie: We can do that – we just have to know which printers. Ask Pathology to log the issues with the service desk.

Satisfied, Richard went back to Pathology and spoke with Dav and Mindy.

Richard: It's all sorted. All you have to do is tell the IT service desk which printers have a problem and they will arrange to fix them.

The next day, Dav called Richard.

Dav: I have called IT to tell them about three printers that need resetting. They won't log the request because I don't have the printer ID numbers. So we are back to square one.

Richard: And can't you get the ID number?

Dav: I'd have to ring all three wards to ask them. It's not my job.

Richard leaves what he is doing again, and wearily goes off in search of Julie.

Richard: Julie, I have finally got Pathology to call the service desk to log these printer problems. They give them the location but your team won't log the call without an ID number. Please can you do something to help us resolve this?

Julie: OK, I'll give special dispensation – for this situation only – and tell my team to log the calls without the numbers, so we can help you.

Richard thanked Julie and walked back to his office, shaking his head, and thinking to himself, surely there has to be a better way …

Introduction

Do you struggle to balance all the demands on your time? Do you sometimes feel that you aren't achieving all that you'd like to? Wherever you look, are there problems to fix? If so, this book is for you.

We originally developed the Five-Minute Coach for managers. We were hearing that life was tough. From senior managers to team supervisors, no matter the size or sector of organisation, the common themes we encountered were long hours, high stress and far too little time out of work to get body and mind in balance, never mind achieve personal goals. That was a few years ago and, as we write this book, it seems that in general things haven't improved. In fact, with the current pressures on resources, competition for market share and increasing globalisation, people are struggling more than ever to maintain their personal and professional effectiveness.

Not so the managers – and others – who have embraced the Five-Minute Coach. They no longer fight fires constantly. They are getting much better results as others take ownership of issues where appropriate. Their approach to work has become more proactive and less reactive; and they are creating opportunities to get a strategic perspective and make a real difference.

As the name suggests, the Five-Minute Coach is an approach to coaching. Increasingly, people find a coaching style of influencing and leading much more effective than controlling and directing. The challenge individuals find though is that coaching just seems to take too long – until now. This book introduces you to a technique of coaching that's ideal for busy people who need to get results swiftly.

Developing the skills

Once you've learned the Five-Minute Coach technique, you'll find it becomes very easy to employ in your working day to make a difference in as little as five minutes. To build that flexibility you need to get to grips with the whole framework, such that you can run a formal coaching meeting with it. A full session does last more than five minutes, although it's still very fast.

After that you'll find yourself using Five-Minute Coach questions in conversations and meetings, and creating positive change around you as a result. Before long, coaching becomes integrated into day-to-day communications between you and your colleagues and a coaching culture emerges.

What it does

The Five-Minute Coach helps people to make a step change in the way they work, which in turn leads to significantly improved performance, in two simple ways:

1   **Delegating.** The process ensures that problems are delegated to their rightful owners. Rather than rescuing others, you relinquish responsibility and return issues back to those who raise them. Often the person who knows most about the problem is best placed to resolve it. With this approach you enable people to take responsibility, to devise solutions, to innovate and to make decisions. Meanwhile, you create the time to think and act differently, and make a more useful contribution yourself.

2   **Revolutionising thinking.** You establish a shift from problem-thinking to an outcome focus. Solving a problem can create a result that is quite different from that generated when attention is on an outcome – what we want to have happen. This doesn't involve ignoring problems; rather you have a new, effective method of moving beyond a problem.

Before long this step change becomes embedded. People start to consider outcomes rather than raising problems. They know they can take ownership and choose when to ask for help – or coaching. Meanwhile, managers stop fixing everything themselves, coach where necessary and get a whole new perspective on the work they are doing. Stress reduces, performance improves and everyone benefits.

Clean questions

The Five-Minute Coach has its roots in Clean Language, a methodology for working with individuals first developed for use in psychotherapeutic settings. Its originator, David Grove, developed the concept of 'clean' questions[1] – those which contain the minimum of assumptions and none of the questioner's ideas, thoughts or suggestions. These questions direct attention to the interviewee's own words and deepen and develop her thinking.

James Lawley and Penny Tompkins studied and further developed Grove's approach, creating Symbolic Modelling,[2] described in detail in their book, *Metaphors in Mind*.[3] Thanks to this work and the training and support they have given to us and many others over the last decade and more, Clean Language is now used in many settings, from business to communities, schools to hospitals, charities to homes. You can discover more about Clean Language by visiting www.cleanlanguage.co.uk (see also Chapter 13).

'Clean' questions, the principles of Clean Language and the structure of Symbolic Modelling, including Lawley and Tompkins's Framework for Change,[4] are at the heart of the Five-Minute Coach. We have taken key clean questions and built a framework that is easy to learn, quick to use and effective at changing the way people think and work.

---

1 Grove, D. (1998). The Philosophy and Principles of Clean Language. Available at www.cleanlanguage.co.uk/articles/articles/38/1/.
2 See Chapter 13 for other opportunities to access information on Symbolic Modelling and Clean Language.
3 Lawley, J. and Tompkins, P. (2000). *Metaphors in Mind: Transformation through Symbolic Modelling*. Developing Company Press.
4 Lawley, J. and Tompkins, P. (2012). A Framework for Change. Available at www.cleanlanguage.co.uk/articles/articles/313/1/.

How to use this book

This book is designed to help you learn how to use this pragmatic and impactful approach to coaching to change the way you work and improve the results you get.

Chapters 1 and 2 describe the Five-Minute Coach and what you need to do to get started. Chapters 3–7 then lead you through the five stages of the process, step by step. To learn the coaching approach you'll need to read them in order – at least initially. You'll discover that these chapters include the Five-Minute Coach questions and guidance on how to use them, complete with examples. You'll find tips, troubleshooting and practice activities, as well as ideas on how you can use the questions in five-minute conversations once you have learned to coach this way.

Then you'll find chapters to dip into when you want to learn more. Chapters 8 and 9 give you guidance on how to handle unexpected responses when coaching. Chapter 10 has some exercises to help you practise your skills. Chapter 11 tells you how the Five-Minute Coach is being used in practice. Chapter 12 explains more about coaching. Chapter 13 includes a list of resources should you want to take your journey of discovery with the Five-Minute Coach further.

Book conventions

Gender

At certain points in the book, to emphasise the importance of the coachee's role in the process, we refer to a coachee by gender (i.e. he or she). We use one pronoun only to make it easier to read, so for example, in the 'Five-Minute Stage in brief' sections at the start of Chapters 3–7, we have made the coachee female through all five. Elsewhere, we alternate gender from one chapter to the next – after all, this book *is* relevant to all!

Question structure

Much of the book is devoted to helping you to ask structured, 'clean' questions from the Five-Minute Coach. So you need a way to recognise, quickly, which part of the question stays the same and which varies depending on what your coachee has said. To help you, the part of the question that stays the same is in bold text, while square brackets indicate which of the coachee's words to insert, and where. For example:

And when [last answer], *then* **what happens?**

requires you to insert the answer the coachee gave to the previous question in the part of the question indicated within the brackets.

Five-Minute conversations

The instructions in this book are, in the main, presented in a way to help you learn the skills of using the Five-Minute Coach to coach formally. Once you have practised coaching in this way, and are ready to use Five-Minute Coach questions informally in everyday conversation, you'll find out how to do this, and where they might be useful, at the end of Chapters 2 – 7 and read some examples in Chapter 11.

Chapters 3–7

These chapters lead you through the five stages of the Five-Minute Coach. There are similarities in their format to help your learning:

 Five-Minute stage in brief – a brief summary of the stage appears at the start of the chapter.

 Five-Minute example – in Chapter 2, you first meet a coach and coachee whose conversation, at each of the five stages, gives you a practical example of how to coach the Five-Minute Coach way. As well as following the stage in each chapter, you can also find that entire coaching conversation in Appendix II.

 Troubleshooting – you'll find a description of how to deal with something out of the ordinary that might occur during each stage. There are many more examples in Chapter 8.

 Five-Minute tips – five helpful tips can be found to support each of the five stages.

 Five-Minute story – to give you a flavour of what is possible, we have included stories from our experience of using the Five-Minute Coach to illustrate each stage. The client information has been anonymised throughout.

 Five-Minute practice – to help you develop your skills each stage has two practice activities for you to try out.

So, if you're a busy person who needs to get results quickly, keep reading to find out how you could benefit from the Five-Minute Coach, as many others have done.

The organisation's experience

Radiography service managers from three different NHS trusts tell of their achievements with the Five-Minute Coach:

"In just over two months there's been a 10 per cent increase in patients seen in Ultrasound; we've saved up to 30 hours of work per month and machine productivity increased from 70–90 per cent.

We've saved up to 28 bed days a month and saved two hours of consultant time per week.

We've increased capacity from 23 to 31 patients per day and patient wait has dropped from 26 days to two!"

The coachee's experience

A teacher coached with the Five-Minute Coach said:

"I found it exciting, frustrating, enlightening, emotional, thought-provoking and empowering. It helped me to get perspective. It allowed me to explore my problem without the usual social communication constraints of being amusing, not droning on, etc. The fact that the coach made little eye contact and gave away nothing through facial expressions was extremely liberating; like being in the room all alone but with a force that was pushing me forward to find the answers. It helped me discover new things. It helped me push further into finding a way of dealing with my problem. It felt very self-generated and improved my self-belief."

The manager's experience

A manager using the Five-Minute coach reported:

"I no longer take work home. I have stopped doing an extra 14 hours per week. We are getting more done and morale in my team is much higher than in the rest of the department. It's a win-win situation."

Chapter 1
Meeting the Five-Minute Coach

Changing the results you get at work by learning how to coach in as little as five minutes starts here. In common with the way most skills are developed, you begin with learning the fundamentals of the process – the principles, the structure and the conventions of the Five-Minute Coach. Then you'll be equipped to run a full coaching session this way *and* you can choose when to use selected Five-Minute Coach questions in everyday conversations to create change for good.

It doesn't take long to learn the basics and get practising. Chapters 3–7 lead you through what you need to do at each stage, as well as how you can use the questions in everyday situations to change thinking, behaviours and performance in as little as five minutes!

The Five-Minute Coach is one of the most non-directive methods of coaching around. It works to people's own strengths and work styles rather than imposing solutions and approaches. Even if you have coached before with other coaching styles and tools, you'll find this approach intriguingly different. This way of coaching generates fast, sometimes unexpected, always interesting and effective results.

The people you coach may be surprised at first, when they realise that you will not advise or suggest solutions to them, or even challenge their ideas. However, they soon come to understand that this style of coaching is all about *them* taking responsibility for resolving problems and achieving goals. They quickly learn to think differently, use initiative and take ownership.

We frequently receive feedback from people coached in this way that it's amazingly powerful. They love the way it helps them to think through things very thoroughly and make considered choices. They experience it as respectful, energising and incredibly practical. The practicality comes not only from the clear structured path mapped out to an outcome, but from the fact that they have personally designed that path built on their own beliefs, strengths and working styles. It *works*.

In this chapter we introduce you to the Five-Minute Coach framework, the questions, a little about how it works and the principles behind it.

The five stages

The Five-Minute Coach is comprised of a series of structured questions. It has five stages, each of which is described in detail in Chapters 3–7. Each stage has a purpose, as follows:

Creating an outcome – what a coachee desires or wants

Stage 1 – Identifying an outcome

Stage 2 – Choosing the best outcome

Stage 3 – Discovering more about the outcome

Creating an outcome is fundamental to the coaching process, so it's the starting point for anyone presenting a problem rather than an outcome. For those who know what they want, and those who are now thinking about an alternative to a problem, Stages 2 and 3 ensure the best outcome is explored and developed.

Generating action

Stage 4 – Action planning

Stage 5 – Motivating to act

Knowing what you want is very different from *having* what you want. This second part of the Five-Minute Coach leads a coachee to create an action plan and find the motivation to actually get started on making things happen.

The Five-Minute Coach questions

The Five-Minute Coach process is quite short – and once you have some experience, quite straightforward. Each stage of the process has its own distinct set of questions, as you will see in the summary of the framework below. No more than five questions need to be learned to complete each of the five stages.

The questions all have some similarities in their format, so once you've practised this slightly unusual style of asking questions, it quickly becomes second nature to ask them in this way.

You'll see that almost all the questions contain square brackets – to guide you as to which words change and which stay the same.

Stage	Purpose	Questions
1	Identifying an outcome	**And what would you like to have happen?**
2	Choosing the best outcome	**And when** [outcome in coachee's words], **_then_ what happens?** **And when** [last answer], **_then_ what happens?** (Repeat question, with each answer, until no new answers emerge) **And** [outcome] **and** [recap all answers], **what are you drawn to most?**
3	Discovering more about the outcome	**And when** [new outcome], **what kind of** [word or phrase from outcome]**?** **And when** [last answer], **is there anything else about** [same word or phrase]**?** **And when** [last answer], **where is/are** [same word or phrase]**?** **And when** [last answer], **whereabouts** [last answer]**?** **And** [last answer]. **Given what you _now_ know, what would you like to have happen?**
4	Action planning	**And what needs to happen for** [final outcome]**?** **And is there anything else that needs to happen for** [final outcome]**?** (Repeat question until you hear first 'no') **And** [final outcome and recap every action point], **and is there anything else that needs to happen for** [final outcome]**?** (Repeat question until you hear second 'no') **And** [final outcome and recap every action point], **and what needs to happen _first_?** **And can** [previous answer]**?**
5	Motivate to act	**And when** [first thing], **_then_ what happens?** (Repeat until coachee is in a positive state and seems keen to act) **And is that a good place to stop?** (Hand over notes)

You can see that almost all of the questions are structured to include a coachee's previous answer. You may also notice that there is no place in the questions for any assumptions or suggestions from the coach. Indeed there are *no* opportunities for you as the coach to ask clarifying questions to help your understanding. In this style of coaching you don't need to understand! The questions are designed to help the coachee, rather than you, understand and discover things about their own thinking. As a result they are known as 'clean' questions – they don't muddy the waters by introducing new thoughts to the coachee.

Here is an example. Your coachee says:

> I feel less stressed.

You ask a question which uses only these words, just changing from 'I' to 'you':

> **And when** you feel less stressed, **then what happens?**

You may ask, is it that simple? Well, yes! And out of this simplicity comes the elegance of minimal intervention with maximum impact. This book guides you carefully through the Five-Minute Coach questions and process. You'll find out how to use each of the five stages in much more detail in chapters 3 – 7. Read the book, start experimenting and practise, practise, practise!

The story of 'and' and 'when'

You'll have noticed that every question you ask in the Five-Minute Coach begins with the word 'and'. This tiny word tells another person that you hear and accept what he has just said. In most Five-Minute Coach questions you follow your 'and' with some of the coachee's words. This helps the coachee to think more extensively about what he has just said.

The word 'when' is also used in many Five-Minute Coach questions. This word puts a coachee's attention on something happening – an event or experience. The value of 'when', combined with 'and', can be demonstrated when you compare the following two statements:

> And when you earn more money, then what happens?

> If you earn more money, then what happens?

The first question presupposes that the person's outcome will be achieved whilst the second marks it as only a possibility, raising doubt. The former helps to guide both the conscious and unconscious mind to fully imagine that the goal has *happened*, which has a positive effect on the coachee. The Five-Minute Coach includes 'and' at the start of all questions, and 'and when' at the start of most, in order to deliver this positive impact to the coachee.

When starting to train in this approach, some Five-Minute Coaches have a tendency to start their questions with the word 'so', rather than 'and'. You'll notice the difference between the impact of 'and' and 'so' when you consider the following two statements:

> And when you get a promotion, then what happens?

> So when you get a promotion, then what happens?

Many people find the word 'so' more judgemental in this context than 'and', which is more accepting. Generally the use of 'so' can interrupt your coachee's flow of thinking. 'And when' is a much more supportive opener to a coaching question, helping to keep the other person's thoughts flowing.[5]

---

5 Tompkins, P. and Lawley, J. (2004). When and How to Use 'When' and 'As'. Available at www.cleanlanguage.co.uk/articles/articles/212/1/.

The Five-Minute Coach principles

Five core principles underlie the Five-Minute Coach. These principles are the powerhouse behind its success. Keeping them in mind will help as you start to learn the process.

1   **Stick with the process**

The questions and process have been carefully developed and honed to provide a powerful and expedient route to create change. Using the process as it is described in this book is essential for your success. Key elements to bear in mind are:

● Ask only the Five-Minute Coach questions

● Use your coachee's precise words within the questions

● Don't introduce any other discussion or dialogue into the coaching

2   **The coachee has all the answers**

No matter what your knowledge, experience or expertise, this process is about the coachee. The questions asked are designed to help him think through issues more comprehensively than before, often uncovering information that was out of his unconscious awareness. So, even when you think you can help the coachee, remember in this situation that you are the coach. It is not your place to offer answers, opinions or advice.

3   **Ownership is with the coachee**

As with all coaching, the person being coached owns the problem or outcome and is therefore best placed to develop what is wanted and determine how to achieve it. He will discover his own route, consistent with his capabilities, beliefs and values, or world view. He then owns the action plan and is responsible for making it happen.

4   **You drive the coaching**

Your role as coach is to guide the other person carefully through the Five-Minute Coach process. You maintain focus on drawing out a meaningful outcome and moving the coachee forwards to achieve it. The coachee, in turn, leads the development of the coaching content.

5   **You create and manage the setting**

You have a critical role in creating the conditions for the coachee to reflect and contemplate issues in ways he hasn't previously considered. You do this by setting the scene at the start, following the Five-Minute Coach process and paying really close attention to the coachee. As you stay calm and collected and manage any uncertainty, you create an environment in which the coachee will gain useful insights and be ready to make the changes he requires.

Manager as coach

If you coach people who report to you, be aware of the potential conflict between coaching and leading. As coach, you facilitate others to accomplish things in their own way. As leader or manager, you help to define other's goals, specify their activity and make them accountable. In addition, you are likely to be responsible for the actions and results of your team members. The key to managing potential conflict is to be aware of which role you are in at any point in time.[6]

Throughout this book you'll read how the Five-Minute Coach is non-directive, with a fundamental principle of not influencing a coachee's thinking or the direction of the coaching. So when you coach you enable the coachee to create his own ideas and plans, and not comment on them.

However, there may be occasions where your knowledge, insights and experience suggest that a coachee's final outcome or action plan

---

6   O'Neill, M. (2000). *Executive Coaching with Backbone and Heart: A Systems Approach to Engaging Leaders with Their Challenges.* Jossey-Bass.

contradicts organisational or team objectives or strategy. We often hear from managers who have been surprised to discover that an issue they thought would need to be addressed resolves itself during the session and needed no further intervention after the coaching finished. However, when this doesn't happen you are duty-bound to discuss the inappropriateness of your team member's plan with him, *after* the coaching, when you re-assume your role as manager.

Should you consider this necessary, make sure that the coachee's action plan or outcome really is inappropriate – not just different from how you would do it. Using this approach means that at least the coachee has had the chance to come up with his own ideas – and by going through the coaching process you may both have learned something that could be useful.

You now have an overview of the Five-Minute Coach framework, including its structured questions and the principles which help to make it a successful way of coaching. In the next chapter you'll learn how to prepare yourself to use the process and how to prime coachees for the way you will work with them.

Chapter 2

Getting Started

You may remember from Chapter 1 that to grow your confidence and proficiency in coaching effectively in as little as five minutes you first need to become accustomed to using the full Five-Minute Coach framework. A formal coaching session takes a little longer, yet often no more than 20 minutes.

When you start to work with the Five-Minute Coach you'll be most successful if you prepare well. You need to prepare yourself *and* the person you are planning to coach. In this chapter we outline what we have found needs to happen for people new to the approach to get off to the best possible start. From there you'll find yourself coaching well and your coachee getting good results.

At the end of the chapter we introduce you to using the Five-Minute Coach conversationally, which you can do once you have learned how it works and had a little practice.

What you need to do

When you work through a full Five-Minute Coach session with a coachee, there are a range of subtle behaviours that you can employ to enhance the experience for the coachee. These nuances make all the difference to the effectiveness of the coaching and so have an important role.

In all there are ten behaviours to remember which we list below. We suggest that when you first start using the Five-Minute Coach you have a copy of Appendix I by your side, which includes the framework and questions and a reminder of the ten Five-Minute Coach behaviours.

Ten important Five-Minute Coach behaviours

1   Pay close attention

2   Use only the Five-Minute Coach questions

3   Avoid the normal rules of conversation

4   Repeat the coachee's words

5   Disregard grammatical rules

6   Take notes

7   Limit eye contact

8   Encourage the coachee

9   Use voice to influence

10 Stay cool, calm and collected

Ten things may seem a lot to remember, but they are all quite straightforward, once you know a little more about them. We will now explore each of them in more detail.

1   Pay close attention

Listening, as a Five-Minute Coach, may well be like no other listening you've done before. It involves paying 100 per cent attention *and* saying nothing for much of the time.

Firstly, pay really close attention to what your coachee says – the precise words you hear. You need to note as many of them down as possible, without changing them, altering grammar or summarising, because you use these exact words in the coaching process.

Secondly, listen to the quality of your coachee's spoken word. What do you detect in the voice? Is there hesitation or ambivalence? Enthusiasm or energy? Frustration or disappointment? Noticing voice tone, pace and pitch will give you information about what to ask about next or *how* to ask your next coaching question.

Finally, while listening, you stay silent. This is essential when your coachee is still in her own thoughts. When you notice her eyes looking at the ceiling or floor, or off into the middle distance, that's a sure sign she is thinking deeply about the question you've asked. You may even hear the coachee say, 'I don't know', and find that when you maintain your silence she finds an answer. People's ability to think deeply and effectively is enhanced by the quality of the attention you pay them.[7]

2   Use only the Five-Minute Coach questions

The Five-Minute Coach questions have been carefully crafted based on years of experience – and they work! As such it's important, when coaching formally, to use the questions just as they're outlined in the framework. It is a specific procedure. Having said that, you'll learn that there are many ways to adapt what you ask the questions about, and *how* you ask them, from one coaching meeting to another. It is here that your true coaching mastery lies.

When you ask Five-Minute Coach questions you direct a coachee's attention. Everyone uses language to express ideas, concepts and beliefs, yet we don't all do this in exactly the same way. Words can have different meanings and promote different emotional experiences from one person to another. So you ask your questions and wait whilst your coachee discovers the information relevant to her.

3   Avoid the normal rules of conversation

One of the more unusual aspects of this style of coaching is that you do not engage your coachee in a dialogue. Your thoughts, ideas and interests are not introduced. Paraphrasing, describing matters as they seem to you or asking questions about things that haven't been explicitly said – all these are for another type of conversation altogether.

---

7   Kline, N. (1999). *Time to Think: Listening to Ignite the Human Mind*. Cassell Illustrated.

Once you've started the coaching process, you don't use the coachee's name. In this way, you help the coachee to stay with her own thoughts, rather than explaining things for your benefit. In effect, you're encouraging her to coach herself.

On a similar note, you never 'help out' by offering words when the coachee seems to be unable to articulate something. Instead, you wait for her to find the word she wants. If there's a silence, learn to become comfortable with it. Your job is to hold the silent space rather than fill it. You don't need to rescue the coachee from any discomfort.

4   Repeat the coachee's words

In the Five-Minute Coach, nearly every question requires you to insert some of the coachee's language into the question.

The accurate repetition of your coachee's words lets her know that you've heard her and enables her to hear what she has just said, but from a different perspective. This usually promotes deeper and more useful insights for the coachee. She finds out new information and moves more easily towards achieving her goal. Most coachees find this a 'gift'.

On occasion, repeating your coachee's words may lead her to decide that she'd like to 'correct' or 'tweak' her answer. You'll discover how important it is for your coachee to have just the 'right' words – the right words for her.

5   Disregard grammatical rules

One of the most challenging aspects of the Five-Minute Coach is that at times you ask a question that in any other conversation would suggest you haven't grasped basic grammar or sentence construction! You insert a coachee's exact words into a question, only to find that it doesn't make much sense to you. Worry not – it makes perfect sense to the other person.

And, contrary to what you may have learned in school, it *is* OK to start a sentence with the word 'and' – or it is when you use the Five-Minute Coach. In fact, all the Five-Minute Coach questions commence with 'and'. And there are good reasons for this (see Chapter 1).

6   Take notes

The whole coaching process becomes much easier when you take notes throughout the session. Write the coachee's words accurately – although most coaches find they need to write in some kind of shorthand, abbreviating words wherever possible to keep up with the coachee's pace. With notes you know where you are in the sequence *and* that you have the precise words you need to structure and form your next question. At the end of the session hand over your notes to the coachee.

7   Limit eye contact

In this style of coaching, limiting eye contact with your coachee is a useful tool that eases the process for both of you. We have a lot of feedback that coachees find it unusual at first, and then discover that limited eye contact is really helpful. The coachee is less concerned with engaging or pleasing you. Instead, she is fully absorbed in her own world, exploring her own thinking more thoroughly. The feeling of pressure to explain everything she says diminishes. She talks to herself as much as – or even more than – she talks to you.

Without the temptation to engage your coachee with empathic eye contact, you stay present with the process. If you don't understand what's just been said, this will be less apparent to the coachee when you are looking at what you are writing rather than at her.

If, like many people, you watch for the clues to know that someone has finished speaking and it's your turn, then here is an opportunity to develop new skills. You can of course keep some of your attention on your coachee, in between writing notes, but you will serve her best if you don't study her intently. Listen and you'll quickly notice the way this person's voice or speech lets you know she's finished. Maybe her voice tails off into silence. Maybe the voice speeds up or sounds more certain. You will detect the signs that she's finished answering.

8   Encourage the coachee

When you use this approach, you influence what your coachee is thinking far less than in any other type of coaching. Your aim is to help her improve how she thinks about her issue and outcome. However, times and opportunities exist for you to gently encourage her to find an answer to a question or to move towards her outcome.

You use encouraging sounds in normal conversation – sounds such as 'hmm', 'uhuh' and others. Use these in the Five-Minute Coach sparingly – in a way that supports your coachee to feel heard and understood; which in turn encourages more responses. Stick to these sounds, avoiding conversational responses such as 'OK', 'really' and 'yes'.

In a formal Five-Minute Coach session, keep your body communication to a minimum. For instance, avoid gesturing when you ask questions or repeat the coachee's words – unless you are indicating a location where the coachee has gestured. Only in Stage 5 of the process (see Chapter 7) might you choose to use your own body language to encourage your coachee – by smiling, nodding or changing posture.

9   Use voice to influence

Be assured that you can develop real skill in the Five-Minute Coach through the effective and flexible use of your voice. You do so much more when coaching this way than just repeating words and predetermined questions.

Your tone, for example, demonstrates that you are interested in, and curious about, what the coachee says. Your tone of voice should reinforce the coachee's statements as if you fully believe them to be true, rather than suggest you are questioning their accuracy.

Adding emphasis to certain words in the questions directs the coachee's thinking and helps in finding an answer. A simple change of emphasis often creates a different experience for the coachee.

Your pace and energy can be used to influence the coaching too. Slowing down the speed with which you ask your questions creates the time and space for the words to be heard and reflected on.

10   Stay cool, calm and collected

The most important thing to manage through a Five-Minute Coach coaching session is you! When you remain calm and collected your coachee has a very good coaching experience. By listening attentively and remaining composed, you improve the coachee's confidence that she's being heard and accepted, which encourages her to reflect more comprehensively. Should your coachee say something that takes you aback, just 'Keep calm and carry on!' Indicate through your manner that the coachee's response is normal. Stick with the process, asking the questions relevant to the stage of coaching you have reached.

If you receive other unexpected responses, like the coachee not having an answer or stating she doesn't understand the question, stay cool. There are a whole range of responses you may adopt, and you'll find these explained in Chapter 8.

Prepare to coach

If you are planning to run a full coaching session with someone at work, there are three important checks to make before you start:
(1) Are you the right person?
(2) Is coaching what's needed? and
(3) Have you agreed a time and place?

1   Are you the right person?

Make sure you both agree that you are well-placed to coach this individual. Check first whether there might be any potential conflicts of interest or issues around confidentiality. For example, might the coachee want to work on initiating a project you have already made a stand against?

When you both work in the same organisation, there can be times when information disclosed in a coaching session may cause a conflict of interest. Ideally you will offer your coachee complete confidentiality, as long as anything disclosed in the coaching is not illegal or unsafe. If there are any conditions other than these when you might have to breach confidentiality, make sure these are made explicit ahead of the coaching. For instance, if you are the human resources director and a coachee reveals that she wants to leave the business, you may be obliged to take that information into account when planning a restructure. The coachee should know where she stands before you get started.

2   Is coaching what's needed?

Have an explicit discussion about whether coaching is what's required. If the other person approaches you with an outcome or goal, or she wants to solve a problem, then coaching is certainly a useful route. If she wants to move responsibility for a problem onto you – looking for you to resolve it, and that is not appropriate – coaching can be useful.

On the other hand, if the other person is seeking your expert advice, wants to influence you to think like her or is just off-loading, then coaching is unlikely to be appropriate.

In addition, there are a range of topics and issues that are not appropriately handled through coaching. For instance, a coachee may wish to talk about matters related to mental health. If you come across anything that indicates a need for specialist therapeutic or psychological support, refer the coachee to seek an appropriate service.

These can usually be accessed via occupational health schemes and general practitioner services.

3   Have you agreed a time and place?

It's helpful to plan a coaching session at least a little ahead of time. This means you can be prepared for the session and your coachee has already started to think about what she wants to achieve. It allows you to find a suitable location – ideally a quiet space, away from other people and free from interruptions.

At the meeting

Finally we come to the meeting itself. You are ready and prepared with your copy of Appendix I and your pen and paper. Now you just have to know what to do!

It's important to set up the coaching session so that the coachee is comfortable with the process. You start by giving her a choice of seating and then, if you are coaching her with the Five-Minute Coach for the first time, explain how the process works and what will happen.

- **Ask where the coachee would like to sit.** Whilst you are both standing, and before either of you puts anything down, ask your coachee to choose where she'd like to sit. This enables her to find a spot where she will be best placed to think well. Then ask her where she'd like you to sit. This already demonstrates that she truly has a leading role in the coaching.

- **Tell her about this style of coaching.** Give a brief introduction to the fact that this coaching will have a somewhat different feel from everyday conversations. Explain that you will not give as much eye contact as usual, nor offer feedback, make comments or suggestions.

- **Mention note-taking.** Inform your coachee that you will take notes throughout the session to help you to coach her. Explain that you'll hand them over at the end of the meeting.

- **Reinforce confidentiality.** Remind your coachee that anything she says is confidential, unless it is something that's illegal or unsafe, or meets any other criteria for breach of confidentiality that you discussed in advance.

- **Give guidance.** Make the coachee aware that you'll be asking coaching questions and should she find some of the questions unusual, she can simply trust whatever answers emerge for her.

  Also, make it clear that once you've started the coaching you will not answer any questions. Offer the opportunity for her to raise any concerns she has now.

Five-Minute example

It's time to meet Amira and Chris. Amira leads a very busy department, with lots of cutbacks in resources but no let-up in demand for services. She spends most of her day dealing with her direct reports and the issues and problems they have, until she discovers the Five-Minute Coach. So, one day, when Chris came to her with a list of complaints and problems, rather than getting embroiled in the usual discussion, Amira agreed a date and time for a formal coaching meeting.

Since this is an ongoing relationship, Amira opens the meeting by explaining that she's just learned a new way of coaching and would like to use it with Chris. Having said that, she begins like this:

Amira: And where would you like to sit (gesturing around the space)?

Chris: (Sits down)

Amira: And where would you like me to sit?

Chris: Hmm – over there? (Chris points and Amira sits down)

Amira: Let me explain a little about this coaching. My job is to help you to explore your issue, work out what you want and how you are going to achieve it. I won't be offering you ideas or suggestions as to how to do it. You'll soon find that this isn't like a normal conversation or even any coaching session you may have had before. I won't look at you much, and I won't make any suggestions or comments about what you say.

I will be taking notes to help me remember what you've said. And at the end, I'll give you all the notes.

Anything you say is confidential, unless it's illegal or unsafe.

If I ask you any questions that seem unusual or odd, just answer with the first thing that comes to mind.

Once we start, I won't answer any questions as that will interrupt the flow. So ... is there anything you'd like to ask me now?

Chris: This definitely sounds like something new! OK, I'll give it a try.

Amira has set up the coaching meeting and explained how it works to Chris. Find out what happens next in Chapter 3 when Amira moves to Stage 1 of the Five-Minute Coach.

Five-Minute conversations

Once you're familiar with the Five-Minute Coach framework and have used it to coach, you can use the questions in day-to-day conversations. You may find yourself listening to other people in quite a different way. You'll notice more occasions when they are talking about problems, or what they want when they seem stuck and when they are asking for help. You'll also be aware of when it might be useful to help them explore an issue rather than fix things for them or join in with their complaints.

The Five-Minute Coach questions interrupt our usual process of trying to make meaning out of what someone else is saying. In conversation, we often don't realise we've 'filled in the gaps' using our own knowledge,[8] and so our questions may be based on our assumptions of what the other person meant. Using the Five-Minute Coach questions with others means we stop making things up.

When you use the Five-Minute Coach questions conversationally the basics of the technique are still essential:

- Use the prescribed Five-Minute Coach questions
- Pay attention and listen well
- Use the other person's words
- Hold fire with your own advice and thoughts

You'll read more about how to do this in Chapters 3–7. For now, be aware that using the questions in an informal setting is similar and yet different from what you do in a more formal coaching meeting.

Some things will be different in an informal context. For instance, you:

- Don't take notes
- Maintain good eye contact
- Make a mental note of the other person's words for your next question
- Keep your voice tone, volume and pace matched to the other person's
- Maintain the whole experience as a 'normal' conversation

A note of caution regarding using the Five-Minute Coach questions conversationally. Be careful about where you are. Think about whether there are any issues around confidentiality or the other person's willingness to open up if you are

---

8 Sullivan, W. and Rees, J. (2008). *Clean Language: Revealing Metaphors and Opening Minds*. Crown House Publishing.

in a public space. In addition, take care that she is open to exploring this issue right now. It's easy to get carried away with your desire to help and you may not always have the person's implicit permission to do so.

You'll find out more about when Five-Minute conversations can be useful in the following chapters.

Identifying an Outcome

"Through the Five-Minute Coach I discovered I was focusing on the wrong thing. The coaching helped me to think differently about what I wanted and now I'm making great progress. Amazing!"

Stage 1: Identifying an outcome	**And what would you like to have happen?**

Five-Minute Stage 1 in brief

Your job as coach in this first stage is to help the coachee establish her outcome – what she wants. Once you're ready to coach, and you've introduced the session as outlined in Chapter 2, you begin with your first Five-Minute Coach question. Ask slowly and deliberately:

And what would you like to have happen?

This question is designed to focus your coachee's mind very clearly on what she wants – an objective or outcome – rather than thinking about an issue or problem that she has. Of course, some people tend to think in terms of outcomes anyway. If your coachee is one of these, and immediately tells you what she wants, move on to Stage 2. If, instead, you hear about a problem, or what she doesn't want, then this chapter shows you how to handle it.

For example, if the answer is:

Coachee: I just don't want to keep taking work home every evening.

Coach: **And when** you don't want to keep taking work home every evening, **what would you like to have happen?**

Coachee: I really want an admin day in the office every couple of weeks.

The coach noticed that this is a problem rather than an outcome and so repeated back some of the coachee's original statement before asking the Five-Minute Coach question again. Notice the coach doesn't suggest other ways of handling the workload problem. If you're a serial problem-solver this valuable question could well be the key to breaking your habit! You're starting your journey to becoming a committed coach.

Just moving someone's thinking from a problem to an outcome – from something *unwanted* to something *wanted* – is very potent. The way the person considers the issue changes. Now both her conscious and unconscious thoughts evolve and adapt. And guess what? That kind of change stimulates *more* change.

Discovering Stage 1

This first stage of the Five-Minute Coach is all about discovering what someone wants or would like to have. Some people know what they want. Others have a much better idea of what they don't want – their problems. Your first goal when coaching is to ensure you find out what the coachee *wants*.

The problem with solving problems

If you have days where all you seem to do is hear about problems, fix problems and advise other people on how to tackle problems, then you're not alone.

In the organisations we work with we constantly notice managers dealing with problems. Of course, that may be a part of the job, but sometimes it just takes over. Problem-solving becomes part of the culture to such an extent that people sometimes don't notice that they're not doing what they were employed to do. As a result, there is less time for activities like planning, streamlining processes, developing talent, creating vision, increasing effectiveness and efficiency, communicating with stakeholders and improving results. Problem-solving rules!

So, one problem with solving problems is that it can get in the way of working strategically, proactively and creatively. Another problem is something you've probably heard before – today's solution can often become tomorrow's problem. The customer service centre that has more calls than it can answer transmits a message asking people to call back at a different time. This reduces the waiting times right *now*, but later all those people call back and recreate the problem at a different time, or worse, don't call back and go to a competitor. The service centre develops a new solution – it puts on more staff, but they're not fully trained. This means they have to keep referring to expert staff for guidance, slowing down not only their own call-handling time but reducing the availability of the expert staff to answer calls. Again, the solution has not solved the problem.

The impact of an outcome

Problem-thinking is sticky! When you think about a problem it's easy to become stuck thinking about, and around, the problem. If, instead, having noticed the problem, you then change your focus to think about how you'd like it to be – you have an outcome. Once you start to think about an outcome, you are thinking differently and have more options and alternative behaviours. In short, things start to become unstuck.

When someone brings you a problem, and you coach him to identify an outcome, the coachee starts thinking about moving out of the problem in his own way; a way that fits with his existing beliefs, values, personality and preferred way of working. And that way may not be exactly the same as yours – in fact it almost certainly won't be – but it gives him the best possible chance of dealing with *his* problem successfully.

An outcome is expressed in terms of what you *want*. It focuses the mind on a future possibility rather than on the problem. Thinking about an outcome or a goal is like a mental rehearsal. You can't think about it without imagining and feeling the experience of having it. Mental rehearsal is a powerful motivator to start doing things differently in order to achieve your outcome.[9]

Here are some examples of the difference between a problem and an outcome.

Problem	Outcome
I don't want to be late for the meeting.	I'd like to arrive in time for the meeting.
I hate my job.	I'd love a job that makes me happy to get up in the morning.
I really dislike making mistakes.	I'd like to be really good at my job.

---

9 Cooper, L. (2008). *Business NLP for Dummies*. John Wiley & Sons.

The more you direct your attention to outcomes, the less stuck you stay in problems. Of course, *you* may think more about outcomes than problems already. But what about all those people who bring you their issues, challenges and problems? You'll find that by regularly asking them about their outcome, you support them to develop the skills to identify what they want, and get on with doing something about it.

The Five-Minute Coach outcome

You're at the start of a formal coaching session. You've done the Five-Minute Coach introduction and offered the coachee a chance to ask you any questions. Now you begin with the first Five-Minute Coach question, asked slowly and deliberately:

And what would you like to have happen?

You may believe that the coachee has already expressed an outcome or goal for the coaching when you arranged the session. It's more likely that he has talked a lot about the problem – or what to do about the problem. This first question focuses the mind, very clearly, away from the problem and onto what a person wants – an outcome. Ask the question and you may both be surprised by the result.

Ask this first question, *slowly* and *deliberately*, as this helps the coachee to slow down if he is thinking rapidly, calming the mind to reflect more carefully on what he would like. When you first start, notice how difficult you find it to ask *only* this question. With practice, it will become easy and natural.

You may sometimes hear that your coachee wants to *not* have or do something. For example: 'I want to stop having to re-work the reports.' Although what has been said describes stopping or remedying the problem, rather than expressing an explicit outcome,[10]

---

10 Tompkins, P. and Lawley, J. (2000). Coaching for P.R.O.'s. Available at www.cleanlanguage.co.uk/articles/articles/31/

in the Five-Minute Coach you treat this, and every 'want', as an outcome.

Figure 1 shows the steps in Stage 1. Note that if the coachee doesn't immediately express an outcome, you ask the question again. Read 'Five-Minute troubleshooting' later in this chapter to find out more.

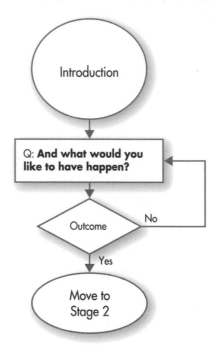

Figure 1: The Stage 1 Five-Minute Coach process

Remember

It may be very tempting to ask something else about what your coachee says – something you believe would be very useful or interesting to know. In fact, the more you know about the coachee's issue, the more likely you will want to bring in some of your expertise. Resist! Sometimes it is easier to coach when you know very little about the subject. This really is a very different conversation from any others you usually have. Your intention here is to encourage the other person to reflect thoughtfully, not to pursue what is of interest to you, to give advice or express an opinion.

If you hear an ambitious outcome – 'I want to be chief executive' – accept it. Even if you believe this apprentice is no more likely to get the job than fly to the moon, acknowledge and work with his outcome. Be aware of showing surprise, horror, amusement or any other emotion in your face and voice tone. Don't challenge the outcome. If it is unrealistic, your coachee will probably work that out at some point later. And discovering something on your own is a hundred times more impactful than hearing someone say you're being 'unrealistic'. If your coachee doesn't find out his outcome is unrealistic, who knows what such an ambitious outcome may achieve.

Really useful questions

The first Five-Minute Coach question, 'And what would you like to have happen?', is very powerful. It puts coachees and their desired outcomes at the centre of things. It allows people to consider what they want. We have coached plenty of people who are rarely genuinely asked what *they* want. So give the coachee plenty of time and space to think about his answer. It may be the most important question you ever ask him. You may notice your coachee becoming more animated and energised as more possibilities are opened up for him to contemplate.

If you're amazed to find that, on occasion, just asking this question is all you need to do to help someone to achieve something new – well, that's the power of this approach. And for those other times, where a bit more support is needed, you have the other questions from the Five-Minute Coach coming up in the following chapters.

Five-Minute **example**

You will remember Amira and Chris from the previous chapter. When Chris brought his problems to Amira, his line manager, she booked a coaching session with him. In Chapter 2, Amira started the coaching with an introduction to the Five-Minute Coach. Now, she takes Chris through this first stage of the coaching. Amira asks the first Five-Minute Coach question, slowly and deliberately.

Amira: **And what would you like to have happen?**

Chris: Now that Jane's gone, and I'm not allowed to replace her, I'd like to know what work I can just *not* do.

Notice that Chris has said what he'd *like* so, in the context of the Five-Minute Coach, this is an outcome and Amira can move on to Stage 2. Find out more about what happens next in Chris's coaching session in the next chapter.

> Chris Coaching   25 October
>
> WLH | Now Jane's gone + I'm X allowd 2 replace, like to know what wk can just not do

Figure 2: Amira's handwritten notes of
Stage 1 coaching session

Five-Minute **troubleshooting**

Most times when you use the Five-Minute Coach outcome question, 'And what would you like to have happen?', you'll hear a response that describes what the other person wants – an outcome.

Occasionally you might find people who are so connected to their problems that they just can't think or talk about anything except the problem. When you ask them what they would like to have happen, you hear even more about what they are struggling with. Or they can tell you what they don't want – but don't express what they'd rather have.

If you have this experience as a coach, there are a couple of tactics. First, ask the question again. Sometimes, a coachee will have an answer the second time around. If all you hear is something about the problem, again repeat your question, picking a word to emphasise within the question, as you think appropriate. As a guide in this situation, asking, 'And what would you *like* to have happen?' often helps the coachee shift to an outcome. Don't concern yourself about the repetition of the question. It often helps to focus the other person's thinking.

If, after at least three iterations you still haven't got an outcome, your second tactic is to focus the coachee with the question: 'And what would you like instead?' For example, Fraser brings his problem to his supervisor, Sean, who uses the Stage 1 Five-Minute Coach question as a standalone, informal question to get him to focus on what he wants:

Fraser: The divisional managers are causing me big problems.

Sean: **And when** the divisional managers are causing you big problems, **what would you like to have happen?**

Fraser: I just can't get the monthly reports out in time when I don't get the figures from the divisional managers until the night before reporting.

Sean: **And when** you can't get the monthly reports out in time, **what *would* you like to have happen?**

Fraser: I'm sick of chasing them up. They know when I need the info.

Sean: **And when** you're sick of chasing them up, **what would you *like* to have happen?**

Fraser: I don't want to be working late into the night, doing it all last minute, making mistakes because there's no time to check it all.

Sean: **And when** you don't want to be working late into the night, doing it all last minute and making mistakes, **what would you like instead?**

Fraser: I want to build in time so that I can create the reports easily – and accurately.

Notice here that it takes Sean a few attempts to elicit the outcome Fraser wants – but his persistence is rewarded.

Remember, it's important to persevere and pursue an outcome that describes what a person wants, rather than what he doesn't want. With a clearly stated outcome change is much more likely to happen.

 # Five-Minute tips

1   Use the Stage 1 Five-Minute Coach question *only*.

2   Let silence be your friend. If someone doesn't respond immediately, wait until he does.

3   Don't get drawn into conversation about the problem.

4   Make sure you work on an outcome that your coachee can do something about. 'I want my boss to give me a promotion' is unlikely to be something the coachee can make happen directly. 'I want to show my boss how capable I am so that she promotes me' is under his control. If you hear an outcome that you think might be outside the coachee's sphere of influence, you can check your impression with the 'And can …?' question normally used only in Stage 4 (see FAQ 23 in Chapter 8).

5   Don't comment on or contribute as a coachee defines his outcome.

Five-Minute **practice**

Sharpen your ear for hearing the difference between what someone doesn't want – a problem – and what he *does* want – an outcome. Listen in as people talk, at work, on the train, even on the TV or radio. Listen for phrases that will give you a strong clue as to whether someone is thinking in terms of a problem or an outcome.

Here are some examples to listen out for:

Problem	Outcome
I don't want ...	I want ...
I hate ...	I like ...
I'm sick of ...	I'd love ...
I can't carry on ...	I wish ...

Now listen to yourself – what you say to others and what you say to yourself. (Don't worry, we all talk to ourselves!) Do you think and talk more about what you don't want or what you do want?

Five-Minute **story**

Sinead, a marketing manager, came to Lynne for coaching. She explained how, the previous week, she'd prepared a presentation to make to her sales colleagues as part of an all-day meeting. The night before the meeting, Sinead spent a couple of hours practising her 30-minute talk in front of her bedroom mirror. She knew her stuff perfectly, and her supporting materials were interesting and informative.

By the day of the presentation, Sinead was paralysed with nerves. Nauseous, with stomach pains, she was terrified of presenting to her colleagues. At the last minute, she asked her line manager to step in, unprepared, and deliver her material to the audience. This wasn't the first time! Sinead looked dejected as she sat in the coaching session. Head hung low, with a weary-sounding voice, her body seemed to crumple into the chair.

Sinead's conclusion was: 'I just *can't* present. It makes me ill with fear and I just look so *stupid*.' Lynne asked: 'And what would you like to have happen?'

Sinead said: 'I want to stand in front of my peers and give them the information they need. I want to stop worrying about making a fool of myself – after all I'm not making a speech to Parliament. And most of all, I really want to be able to explain the great work my team is doing to support the sales guys to achieve their goals. My team deserves the recognition – and I want the sales team's respect.'

This was quite a long answer and, as she continued to speak, Lynne noticed changes in Sinead. She was becoming more energised, talked faster and with more determination. Her voice was stronger. Lynne allowed the silence to develop, so Sinead could think further if she wanted to. Suddenly Sinead exclaimed: '*Oh no!* Of course, that's it. What I want is my colleagues' respect. And by getting all wound up and backing out of my responsibilities, like my presentation, I am most likely losing their respect. How stupid!'

For Sinead, her insight into her outcome, and how she was getting in her own way of achieving it, was enough for her to start making changes. Lynne didn't need to lead her through the full Five-Minute Coach framework on this occasion as Sinead was already working out what she needed to change, and how. When the next quarterly sales meeting came round she made her presentation, received good feedback, and has never looked back.

 ## Five-Minute **practice**

Here's an experiment. Pick two days in the coming week where you aim to use the 'And what would you like to have happen?' question at least 12 times in the day. It doesn't matter where or when. You'll find it's a great information-gathering question the more you use it.

If you are in a meeting, as people arrive, ask them what they'd like to have happen. When someone raises an objection to something, ask the same question. When someone is having a moan at the coffee machine, yet again, ask!

Five-Minute Coach Framework so far

So far you've learned about the first stage of the Five-Minute Coach: helping someone to establish an outcome rather than being stuck in a problem.

1	Identifying an outcome	**And what would you like to have happen?**

Five-Minute conversations

As you are aware, the Five-Minute Coach can be used in a whole range of informal situations, as well as formal coaching. You get great results – in as little as five minutes – just by using any one or more of the powerful Five-Minute Coach questions.

The Stage 1 question can be asked easily in conversation. When you hear someone complain, or talk about a problem, or sound like they are frustrated with a situation, just ask, 'And what would you like to have happen?' You'll be amazed at the impact of encouraging people to think about what they want rather than what's wrong. Here are just a few of the things that are achievable with this question.

- **Getting problems fixed by the right people.**
  The 'right' person to solve a problem is the person experiencing it, or indeed the person who decides something is a problem due to the way he thinks about the issue. Although they may not have caused it, in the

majority of cases that person understands most about the problem, its complexities and its impact. The Stage 1 Five-Minute Coach question enables individuals to start tackling problems in their own way.

- **Stopping people in their tracks when grumbling or complaining.** Whinging, moaning and blaming is found in pockets of most organisations. Sometimes it becomes culturally entrenched, with lots of projection of everything that's wrong onto 'them', which can be bosses, customers, suppliers, other departments and so on. When you ask, in response to a tirade of complaints, 'And what would you like to have happen?', you direct the other person's attention beyond being stuck in the problem and towards change.

- **Changing stuck thinking and introducing new possibilities.** The question nudges people to stop thinking about a difficulty and to start considering alternatives. Instead of going around and around attempting to analyse a problem, contemplation of what a person would rather have is often enough to start change happening.

- **Freeing up your time**. The more you ask this question of colleagues and team members, the faster they become accustomed to thinking about outcomes, and the less they lean on you for providing solutions. Quite quickly you find people presenting you with far fewer problems, leaving you to pay attention to matters on your own agenda.

- **Finding out more information.** Asking, 'And what would you like to have happen?' in general conversations is an invaluable way of getting to know more about what someone else wants or is thinking. It's useful in any discussions where you want to offer a service or help to someone, because it gives you much better quality information with which to target your offering. One of the most useful features of this question is that it stops you thinking you know what the other person wants, and then acting on your assumption.

- **Moving your own thinking beyond a problem you have.** When you find yourself caught up in circular thinking and not making progress with something, you too may find that you are just not outcome focused enough to make a shift. Once you know what you actually want you may start to make headway.

- **Opening meetings.** When you ask each attendee at the start of a meeting what they would like to have happen, everyone's objective for the meeting is voiced. Attendees gain a shared understanding. It is an invaluable way to improve the effectiveness of a meeting by eliminating assumptions.

- **Empowering people.** By not taking on others' problems, yet facilitating them to think about an outcome they want, you encourage and empower them to believe they can make change happen.

- **Dealing with formal complaints.** By not immediately offering solutions, and asking this question instead, you find out what the person wants. It may be less than you'd have offered!

Choosing the Best Outcome

"At one point I felt I had reached a conclusion and was fed up with the coach for continuing (God, if she says, 'And then what happens?' one more time I'll scream ... can't she see I've done?) but then made a far greater breakthrough by carrying on, resulting in a real eureka moment. Great coaching!"

Stage 2: Choosing the best outcome	**And when** [outcome in coachee's words], **then what happens?**
	And when [last answer], **then what happens?** (Repeat question, with each answer, until no new answers emerge)
	And [outcome] **and** [recap all answers], **what are you drawn to most?**

Five-Minute **Stage 2** in brief

The essence of the Five-Minute Coach is identifying an outcome – the best outcome from the coachee's perspective. Having already discovered the outcome (what someone wants) at Stage 1, now you help your coachee to explore what happens next – the consequences and impact of achieving the outcome.

Taking your coachee's outcome, elicited at Stage 1, ask:

> **And when** [outcome in coachee's words],
> *then* **what happens?**

Write down the exact words of the answer, using your own shorthand if necessary, and ask:

> **And when** [last answer], *then* **what happens?**

Now you're on a roll. Keep repeating at least the key words of the answer you've just been given, and ask the same question until you hear the coachee repeat answers, or the answers include words like 'happy', 'fulfilled' or you hear the equivalent of 'That's all!'

At this point, repeat *all* the answers, in sequence, to your coachee as part of the following question:

> **And** [outcome] **and** [recap all answers],
> **what are you drawn to most?**

You'll find that your coachee readily chooses an outcome from this list. It may be the same as, or different from, what she first said she wanted. It may be one of her answers or a combination of things she has discovered at this stage. Or she may even have realised that what she thought she wanted was not what she wanted at all and may articulate an alternative outcome! Whatever the result, accept the answer as what the coachee *now* knows she wants.

Example: Starting with a Stage 1 outcome

Coachee: I want to make a good presentation.

Coach: **And when** you make a good presentation, ***then* what happens?**

Coachee: Then my ideas will be taken seriously.

Coach: **And when** your ideas are taken seriously, ***then* what happens?**

Coachee: I'll get the backing to start to make the changes.

Coach: **And when** you get the backing to start to make the changes, ***then* what happens?**

Coachee: Costs will come down – up to 8 per cent.

Coach: **And when** costs come down – up to 8 per cent, ***then* what happens?**

Coachee: I'll be really happy.

Coach: **And** you make a good presentation, your ideas are taken seriously, you get the backing to start to make the changes, costs come down – up to 8 per cent, and you're really happy. **What are you drawn to most?**

Coachee: Getting backing to start to make the changes.

Discovering Stage 2

Exploring consequences

In a busy world where you're constantly rushing to get things done, it's very tempting to 'just get on with it'. In many organisations activity is applauded, no matter whether it's in pursuit of a useful goal.

One of the key differences between the Five-Minute Coach and other coaching approaches is that three of the five stages of the framework are all about the outcome. You'd be forgiven for thinking this is excessive. Yet in our experience, it's what makes this coaching so effective.

In Stage 2 you coach someone to explore the consequences of what she thinks she wants – what happens once she's achieved her outcome. This provides a lot more information to your coachee – often new things come to mind. The coachee is then better placed to decide whether to stick with her original outcome, phrase it more appropriately or come up with something different.

Choosing outcomes

When you coach someone through this process, you may find that once the coachee has identified the consequences of an outcome, one of the consequences becomes more attractive than the original outcome.

For example, Stephen's initial outcome is: 'I want to get all my paperwork organised and filed.' As he thinks it through, the consequences are 'I can work faster and easier' and then 'I can leave the office at a sensible time each night, instead of late.' The upshot may be that Stephen chooses 'leaving the office at a sensible time' as his ultimate outcome. When he pursues this outcome, Stephen may find there are other things he needs as well as getting his paperwork organised and filed.

Alternatively, when exploring an outcome in this way, coachees sometimes uncover some less attractive implications – things they hadn't thought about. For example, Gail, an account manager, initially wanted to manage a team of people. When she considered 'And then what happens?', she quickly realised that she'd be spending a lot more time in the office. That would mean less time with clients, where she was at her best – and happiest. Gail completely revised her outcome to 'I want a more strategic element to my role, so I can build long-term partnerships with key clients.' It's easy to see how Gail's coaching went in quite a different direction than she'd expected.

Coaching to identify the best outcome

When you lead your coachee through the second stage of the Five-Minute Coach you give her the time to slow down, reflect thoroughly and identify the implications of achieving her outcome. When you ask the question:

> **And when** [outcome in coachee's words], **then what happens?**

insert the coachee's exact words between the square brackets in the question as indicated. Put a slight emphasis on the word 'then'. Pause to hear the answer – without interrupting – creating a quiet space for her to give a considered response. When you hear the answer, write down as much as you can – at least key words and phrases. Then take the answer, and ask again:

> **And when** [last answer], **then what happens?**

As you repeat this question, ask it with curiosity and respect to help your coachee's flow of thinking – and ensure she doesn't feel interrogated!

Continue to ask this question, writing down each answer in turn, until the coachee begins repeating herself or tells you she has no more answers. The repetitive nature of your questioning is helpful to the coachee. She starts to predict what you're going to ask next. Knowing the likely question enables her to pay attention to what she may not have been aware of previously.

Next you feed back all the coachee's answers in the following question:

> **And** [outcome] **and** [recap all answers], **what are you drawn to most?**

Again, write down the answer. You'll do more work with this at the next stage. Your coachee may choose her original outcome, or a completely unrelated outcome, as described above. On most occasions the coachee chooses something from the answers to the questions you have just asked.

Figure 3 shows the steps in Stage 2, demonstrating that the first question is asked multiple times.

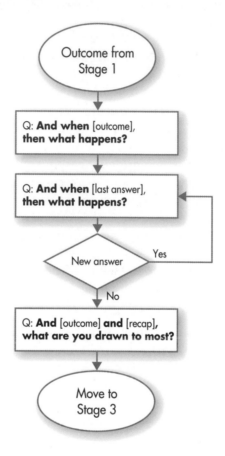

Figure 3: The Stage 2 Five-Minute Coach process

Making changes to coachee's words

It is only in this stage, and Stage 5 of the Five-Minute Coach, that you can – and indeed should – change the tense of what your coachee has said. If the outcome is:

I want to be successful.

Your question is:

And when you *are* successful, ***then* what happens?**

The 'want to be' becomes 'are' when the question is asked. This change suggests that achieving the outcome is possible. Your coachee has to think about having something – in this case 'being successful' – in order to answer your question.

If you didn't change the tense, the coachee wouldn't get the opportunity to explore the consequences of having the outcome. The purpose of Stage 2 is to check that the consequences are desirable, or at least acceptable. Once she has settled that to her own satisfaction she can move confidently in the direction she wants.

You also change one other thing that the coachee says. If you hear 'I', respond in the normal manner by changing the 'I' to 'you'. Sounds obvious, but there are other questions in the Five-Minute Coach framework where you can make *no* further changes – even when what you ask sounds quite ungrammatical. You'll find out more about that in Stage 3.

Remember

Your opinion doesn't matter! As the boss, you may believe wholeheartedly that your coachee is choosing the 'wrong' outcome. Bite your tongue. Wait and see. In our experience, the Five-Minute Coach framework shows just how amazingly resourceful and creative people are.

As you reflect on advice and solutions that you've offered to people in the past, have you ever heard the 'Yes, but …' response? Some people are excellent at working out why someone else's idea won't work for them. The Five-Minute Coach overcomes that by never suggesting a solution (or an outcome). Instead, because the coachee has chosen the way forward, there is a much greater personal commitment to making it work.

Really useful questions

Although a seemingly simple question, 'And then what happens?' is not something you often hear people ask. It's easy to assume that what we think we want, or what we think we should do, will lead to a more positive result than the current situation.

When you ask this question – of others or yourself – assumptions become a thing of the past. Instead you uncover valuable insight into the potential effects of desires, expectations and decisions.

 ## Five-Minute example

You'll remember that Chris has asked his manager, Amira, for help as he's not coping well with the increased workload since losing a member of staff. Amira has coached Chris to find an outcome. Now Amira is using Stage 2 of the Five-Minute Coach to help Chris explore and choose his best outcome.

Amira: **And when** you know what work you can just *not* do, ***then* what happens?**

Chris: Then half my to-do list vanishes and only the important things are left.

Amira: **And when** only the important things are left, ***then* what happens?**

Chris: Then I stay focused. I can go through things easily to work out the priorities, make the connections, skim the folder of non-priority stuff looking only for things that relate to the priorities I'm tackling.

Amira: **And when** you stay focused, work out priorities, make connections, skim the folder looking only for things that relate to priorities, ***then* what happens?**

Chris: Then I meet my deadlines.

Amira: **And when** you meet your deadlines, ***then* what happens?**

Chris: Then people will come to me for my experience. I won't let them down.

Amira: **And when** people come to you and you won't let them down, *then* **what happens?**

Chris: I'll get involved in the more challenging projects and get a good reputation ... and maybe I won't get overlooked when the next departmental manager job comes up.

Amira: **And when** you're involved in more challenging projects, get a good reputation and maybe won't get overlooked when the next manager job comes up, *then* **what happens?**

Chris: Then I do a better job, enjoy it more and I'm on track to move up the career ladder – and earn more!

Amira: **And when** you do a better job, move up the career ladder and earn more, *then* **what happens?**

Chris: Then I'm very happy!

Amira: **And when** you're very happy, *then* **what happens?**

Chris: I should have said I'm very happy *and* successful!

Amira: **And when** you're happy *and* successful, *then* **what happens?**

Chris: Hmm ... nothing else!

Amira: **And** you'd like to know what work you can just *not* do. **And** half your to-do list vanishes and only the important things are left ... you stay focused, you go through things easily to work out the priorities, make the connections, skim the folder of non-priority stuff looking only for things that relate to the priorities you're tackling ... you meet your deadlines ... people come to you for your experience ... you won't let them down ... you get more involved in the more challenging projects and get a good reputation and maybe won't get overlooked when the next departmental manager job comes up ... you do a better job, move up the career ladder and earn more ... and you're very happy. **What are you drawn to most?**

Chris: Focusing, prioritising and meeting important deadlines.

WLH	1/2 my To Do list vanishes + only imp things R left
TWH	Stay focused, can go thru' things easily
	2 wk out priorities, make connections, skim x-priority stuff, lookg only 4 things relate 2 priorities
TWH	Mt my deadlines
TWH	Pple come 2 me. I won't let them down
TWH	Involved in > challenging projs, get gd reputn + maybe X get overlkd when next mgr's job comes up
TWH	Do bttr job, enjoy >, move ↑ career ladder, earn >
TWH	V. happy
TWH	V. happy + successful
TWH	—
TWH	Focusg, prioritising + mtg imp deadlines

Figure 4: Amira's handwritten notes of Stage 2 coaching session

You'll notice a couple of things from this example. Each question begins with 'and'. And Amira repeats some keys words that the coachee has just said, and only *then* asks the Five-Minute Coach question.

Amira was able to jot down most of Chris's words and phrases and so could repeat a lot, though not everything. Using the key words from each point is enough to let Chris hear what he's just said, and allow him the opportunity to change anything.

At the end of this stage, Chris has considered all his answers and selected an outcome which isn't an exact phrase that he's previously used. He has worked out his latest version of what he wants. You can find out what Amira asks him next when you read the following chapter.

Five-Minute **troubleshooting**

Occasionally when going through Stage 2 of the Five-Minute Coach, a coachee might feel uneasy because an outcome has a mix of good and bad consequences. For example, a coachee has developed an outcome in Stage 1 of 'I want a foreign posting.' You ask:

> **And** when you have a foreign posting, **then what happens?**

The coachee responds:

> I'd have some great experience for the future ...
> but I'm worried I'd lose visibility here in head office.
> Then I'd get overlooked for promotion.

Now your coachee has an outcome with a potential problem attached to it. So it's not likely to be exactly what she wants after all. At this point stop asking 'And *then* what happens?' and revert to the Stage 1 question to give her the opportunity to amend the outcome. In this example, you say:

> **And** you'd have some great experience but you're worried that you'd lose visibility and get overlooked for promotion, **and what would you *like* to have happen**?

You have fed back the dilemma and given the coachee the chance to re-think what she wants. As soon as she has a consequence she is happy with, you continue through the Stage 2 questions. In the example, the coachee may decide:

> I'd like a foreign posting *and* maximise my chances for promotion.

You then ask:

> **And when** you have a foreign posting and maximise your chances for promotion, **then what happens?**

You continue to ask the question, as outlined earlier in the chapter, until you get no new answers from the coachee. Then you ask the final Stage 2 question, where you recap her outcome and answers and ask what she is drawn to most. In the unlikely event that the coachee's response at this stage is to select something she *doesn't* want, such as:

> I don't want to lose visibility

you need to ask the question that will focus attention on what she *wants*:

> **And when** you don't want to lose visibility, **what *would* you like to have happen?**

One way or another, your coachee now has an outcome and is ready for Stage 3.

 ## Five-Minute tips

1   Be resolute in using the questions as they are phrased. They really do work!

2   Write down what your coachee says in a coaching session, capturing the words accurately. Make up your own shorthand if necessary, as long as you can read it back.

3   When the coachee refers to 'I', change this to 'you' when you repeat back, as you would do in normal conversation.

4   Amend the tense of what the coachee wants before asking the question. So 'want to have' becomes 'have', and 'want to be' becomes 'are'.

5   If the answers are long and your note-taking can't keep up, relax. Your coachee is likely to be an extravert and more prone

to thinking aloud. As a rule of thumb use the last statement as the answer to include in your next question.

Five-Minute **practice**

Practise the skill of using other people's language by repeating some of their words in a questioning tone. It's as if you are asking a question. Generally the other person will proceed to give you more information, and you have the opportunity to practise your listening skills too!

So when a colleague says something like:

> Recruiting an administrator is taking
> much longer than I anticipated.

Respond with either:

> Much longer?

or

> Recruiting is taking much longer?

Then just listen as your colleague elaborates. Take a week to practise repetition at every opportunity. You'll find your memory and understanding of what others say improves too.

Five-Minute **story**

Ana had for some time been running a community project as well as holding down a job. Yet she didn't have full-time access to a computer or a smart-phone, which limited the hours she could work on certain activities, and meant she didn't have 24-hour access to email. Sometimes urgent work was delayed, but mostly Ana went out of her way to access a computer whenever necessary. However,

Ana's diligence meant she was away from home a lot and the project work took up considerable time.

Ana came to Mariette for coaching. She had identified a clear goal before her coaching session. She wanted to acquire a computer.

To Ana's surprise, repeatedly being asked the question 'And *then* what happens?' led her to realise that, with a computer at hand, she'd be tempted to spend more of her spare time working on the community project – and her commitment was already substantial. She would spend even less time with her family.

This revelation gave Ana a whole new perspective. Working longer hours on the community project was not what she wanted at all. Yet that would have been the consequence of obtaining a computer. With this information, Ana had a complete re-think about how she needed to work more effectively and efficiently to balance the needs of her job, the project *and* her family.

 ## Five-Minute **practice**

Practising the Five-Minute Coach questions from Stage 2 will help you feel confident and sound assured when you use them in coaching.

Next time you're in conversation with someone, in work or else-where, and you are about to comment on a decision the other person has made (you know the sort of thing: 'Really? Are you mad?', or 'Well, I wouldn't do it that way', or 'Have you thought about trying ...?'), stop! Bite your tongue before you comment, and instead ask: 'And *then* what happens?' If the answer warrants it, repeat the question as many times as you think is valuable. Notice the impact you're having. Your goal is to learn something new, not upset friends and colleagues, so back off if you see or hear the other person becoming unhappy with your line of questioning.

Aim to ask the Stage 2 question, 'And then what happens?' for a whole week – ideally with a minimum of three people a day. Notice what happens to your conversations.

Five-Minute Coach Framework so far

Stage	Purpose	Questions
1	Identifying an outcome	**And what would you like to have happen?**
2	Choosing the best outcome	**And when** [outcome in coachee's words], ***then* what happens?** **And when** [last answer], ***then* what happens?** (Repeat question, with each answer, until no new answers emerge) **And** [outcome] **and** [recap all answers], **what are you drawn to most?**

Five-Minute conversations

Just like all parts of the Five-Minute Coach, the main Stage 2 question can be used in many Five-Minute conversations, wherever they happen.

When you use the question informally, you can shorten it to: 'And *then* what happens?' A word of caution: if you use this question conversationally make sure you are only asking it about something somebody wants or something they intend to do.

This really handy question can be used in many situations. Here are a few examples of where we have found it particularly helpful:

- **Identifying unforeseen fallout.** When you hear people telling you they have identified solutions to problems, explore whether they are aware of all the possible consequences of those solutions. Asking, 'And then what happens?' will quickly detect any unintended or undesirable consequences that could result.

- **Discovering the consequences of achieving something you want.** Explore the impact on other aspects of your life, including the impact on others, of your chosen course of action.

- **Eliciting ultimate requirements.** When scoping a project or defining customer needs, getting to the heart of what is being aimed for can be tricky. People will often tell you what they think they want, only to find when it's delivered that it doesn't actually do the job. By discovering 'then what happens', it's much easier to define the full outcome for the piece of work, which may lead to a very different solution.

- **Holding back from giving advice.** It's easy to express an opinion on someone else's goals or proposed course of action. Yet despite your best intentions such commentary often isn't helpful. Asking this simple question allows you to stay very usefully engaged in conversation whilst refraining from giving input.

- **Keeping ownership where it belongs.** When others invite you to make a choice on their behalf, you are inevitably embroiled in any fallout or blame should things not work out. Refrain from making other's decisions by asking, 'And what are *you* drawn to most?'

Chapter 5
The Five-Minute Coach Stage 3

Discovering More

"I found being coached this way stills the mind. Things come forward, and the coaching loosens their stickiness. Then you can speak them, and that makes things attainable."

Stage 3: Discovering more about the outcome	**And when** [new outcome], **what kind of** [word or phrase from outcome]?
	And when [last answer], **is there anything else about** [same word or phrase]?
	And when [last answer], **where is/are** [same word or phrase]?
	And when [last answer], **whereabouts** [last answer]?
	And [last answer]. **Given what you *now* know, what would you like to have happen?**

Five-Minute Stage 3 in brief

Having developed a well-thought through outcome in the first two stages of the Five-Minute Coach, your coachee is now going to discover even more about what she would like to achieve. This deeper knowledge will help refine the outcome still further until it is exactly what the coachee wants.

First repeat the most recent outcome or goal identified in Stage 2. Pick a single word or very short phrase from what the coachee said. Next, ask four core questions to help her learn more about her outcome. The first three questions are asked about the word or phrase you chose from the outcome:

> **And when** [new outcome], **what kind of** [word or phrase from outcome]**?**

> **And when** [last answer], **is there anything else about** [same word or phrase]**?**

> **And when** [last answer], **where is/are** [same word or phrase]**?**

This next question is asked about the answer the coachee just gave you, rather than the word or phrase from the outcome.

> **And when** [last answer], **whereabouts** [last answer]**?**

Remember when asking these questions that your primary role is to help the person you're coaching get more information. So ask the questions just as they're written here, using the actual words of the coachee, even if this makes your question ungrammatical and sound strange. Stick with it: it works! You don't have to understand the question *or* the answer. That's your coachee's job!

At this point, there's one further question:

> **And** [last answer]**. Given what you *now* know, what would you like to have happen?**

Write down the coachee's exact words. The outcome is likely to have changed, even if only subtly, from where it started in this stage.

Example: Starting with a Stage 2 outcome

Coachee: Doing well in my job.

Coach: **And when** doing well in your job, **what kind of** doing?

Coachee: Doing really good work. Feeling fired up.

Coach: **And when** fired up, **is there anything else about** doing?

Coachee: It just happens. I don't have to work at it.

Coach: **And when** it just happens and you don't have to work at it, **where is** doing?

Coachee: It's in my hands.

Coach: **And when** it's in your hands, **whereabouts** in your hands?

Coachee: Hmm ... actually it's in my hands and my heart, with a connection between the two. I don't know where these answers are coming from!

Coach: **And** in your hands and your heart, with a connection. **Given what you *now* know, what would you like to have happen?**

Coachee: To work really well every day.

Discovering Stage 3

Stage 3 of the Five-Minute Coach is all about refinement. The coachee has an outcome or goal, has considered the consequences of having it, and decided whether to change or refine his outcome. Now that he's picked an outcome, your role as coach is to help him explore it further and get a richer understanding of what he wants. This leads to the fine-tuning that's vital before it becomes clear what the coachee *truly* wants.

Exploring qualities and attributes

Stage 3 works with the most recent expression of what the coachee wants, digging deeper into the thinking that lies behind it. He learns more about the outcome and himself. As a result he is able to articulate his outcome very precisely, which improves the quality of the next stages of the coaching.

You ask four core questions to help your coachee find out more about his outcome, before the concluding question pulls all the information together. When you first learn these questions, they may seem strange. Once they're part of your natural repertoire, you'll find yourself using them (well, at least the first three) in all kinds of situations – with the plumber, your doctor, your boss, just about anywhere.

The first two questions in this stage encourage the coachee to think about the attributes or characteristics of one word (or phrase) he has used. If you've asked about 'recognition', he is now directed to think more about what *kind* of recognition and to think about what it means to him and what's important about it. You may well find your coachee has a very different interpretation of the word 'recognition' from yours.

The remaining two questions specifically direct the coachee's attention to a location – which could be in space *or* in time. The answer to 'Where is recognition?' could be in space, such as 'in the office', 'in my salary' or 'in my heart'. It could also be in time such as 'in the future'.

Gathering more information

Begin by choosing any word or very short phrase from your coachee's outcome to use in your first three questions.

The four core questions all have a different, although complementary purpose. Let's look at them in turn. The first question is:

> **And when** [new outcome], **what kind of**
> [word or phrase from outcome]**?**

The second question, which again is applied to the word or phrase you selected from the coachee's outcome, is:

And when [last answer], **is there anything else about** [same word or phrase]**?**

No matter how tempted you may be, don't comment on what you hear or ask other questions that you may feel desperate to ask. That isn't the Five-Minute Coach way. This is your coachee's 'recognition', not yours.

The third question is:

And when [last answer], **where is/are** [same word or phrase]**?**

By now you know the routine. So, continuing the example, ask 'Where is recognition?'

If you're like many of the people who attend our Five-Minute Coach workshops, you may be thinking that this seems an odd question. Lots of words may not *obviously* lend themselves to having a location. The next, fourth, question also sometimes creates hesitancy in the minds of those discovering this coaching approach for the first time.

And when [last answer], **whereabouts** [last answer]**?**

This is the only question from the four not asked of the word or phrase from the outcome, but of the answer to the previous, 'where' question. It's designed to pinpoint more detail. So, in the example, if the previous answer had been 'in the office', you'd ask, 'And when in the office, whereabouts in the office?'

Notice the flow of questions for Stage 3 in Figure 5.

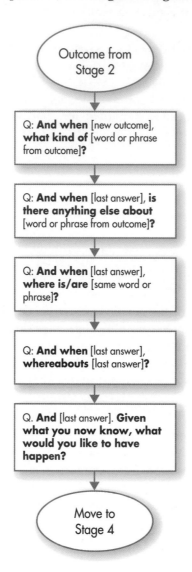

Figure 5: The Stage 3 Five-Minute Coach process

Location, location, location

Usually, 'where' gives you a broad location and 'whereabouts' pinpoints it more accurately. Some people have the opposite experience. Either way the answer is nearly always different. Check it out for yourself by answering the following questions:

> **And where** do you live?

> **And whereabouts** [last answer]?

You may find asking the two location questions uncomfortable on occasions. Yet in most cases your coachee will answer both questions easily. Just occasionally someone might look at you blankly in response to the 'where' or 'whereabouts' questions. Find out how to handle this in the Five-Minute troubleshooting section later in this chapter.

Honing the outcome

Having taken your coachee through the four core questions, you have just one final outcome question to ask:

> **And** [last answer]. **Given all that you *now* know, what would you like to have happen?**

The coachee now has a third opportunity to review, refine and reword his outcome.

Make sure you write down his words accurately. As this is the final outcome or goal it needs to be captured. No matter how long the outcome, write down every word. And if you say it as you write it, your coachee will quickly correct you if you have even the slightest word wrong!

The coachee will most likely have changed his outcome, even if it sounds very similar to the original one. The sequence of words may have changed or maybe a word is different. Any change is likely to be significant to the coachee. Remind yourself that you don't know

– or need to know – what these changes mean. This is your coachee's agenda.

If you're the kind of person who just likes to get on with things, you may be itching to support your coachee to *do* something now. You'll be pleased to know that you're about to spend time action planning, the Five-Minute Coach way, in the next chapter.

Remember

No matter how tempted you are, do not comment on what your coachee says or ask questions you hope would help *you* to understand more. Remember that the meaning and characteristics of the word or phrase you selected are very specific to the coachee, and possibly to the context in which they are currently thinking. It's highly unlikely to match your interpretation of the same word or words. So let go of the need to make sense of the content of the coaching.

Really useful questions

The four core Stage 3 questions help people gain more insight into how they have structured their thinking about things outside of their conscious awareness. They develop more understanding, open up opportunities for change and increase motivation.

Of course they're fabulous information-gathering questions too, used by sales people, school teachers, researchers, parents, trainers, medical and clinical staff – even police officers. Wherever you need more information or find yourself making assumptions about what someone else is saying, ask a Five-Minute Coach question – and be amazed by what you find out.

Five-Minute **example**

Chris and his manager, Amira, concluded Stage 2 of the Five-Minute Coach having explored the consequences of the outcome Chris had originally identified. As a result Chris has rephrased his outcome to 'focusing, prioritising and meeting important deadlines' and Amira is ready to move him through Stage 3, to discover more about his outcome.

Amira: **And when** focusing, prioritising and meeting important deadlines, **what kind of** prioritising**?**

Chris: Standing back, and creating space to think.

Amira: **And when** standing back and creating space to think, **is there anything else about** prioritising**?**

Chris: Yes. It's about what's important, what's urgent. Actually what bits of work will make a difference.

Amira: **And when** it's about what's important, what's urgent, what bits of work will make a difference, **where is** prioritising**?**

Chris: I'm not sure … actually it's in front of me.

Amira: **And when** it's in front of you, **whereabouts** in front of you**?**

Chris: Just here (Chris gestures to a space from left to right of his body, at waist level).

Amira: **And it's there** (pointing to space Chris has just indicated). **Given what you *now* know, what would you like to have happen?**

Chris: I'd like to find it easy to meet my deadlines.

You'll notice Chris has changed his outcome from 'focusing, prioritising and meeting important deadlines'. Amira could have selected any word from Chris's outcome at the start of this stage. She happened to choose 'prioritising'. Find out how Amira coaches Chris through Stage 4, to create an action plan to achieve this amended outcome, in the next chapter.

WKO	Standg back + creatg space 2 think
AE	What's imp, what's urgent, what bits wk will make diff
W	In front of me
WA	Just here
Now	2 find it easy 2 mt my deadlines
WLH	

Figure 6: Amira's handwritten notes of Stage 3 coaching session

Five-Minute troubleshooting

Just occasionally, someone might look at you blankly in response to the 'where' or 'whereabouts' questions. Alternatively he may ask you to explain what you mean.

Let's take the first scenario. If the coachee looks at you blankly, do nothing. You may have your head down, writing notes, or up and looking at him. Either way, stay quiet and wait. Break eye contact if you have it. Then count to 10. Usually the enforced silence supports the coachee to find an answer. He may look confused and even be dismissive about the answer that emerges. Your job is to accept and write down whatever is said. Even when people don't value what they've just said, their answers are usually relevant and appropriate. They just don't know it yet!

The second thing that might occur is that your coachee asks you a question. If you're asked, 'What do you mean?', again don't respond. In Chapter 2 you read about how to set up a Five-Minute Coach session. So before the coaching began you explained that you wouldn't answer questions once coaching had commenced. So stay calm and say nothing. Usually people remember what you said, and then spend some time reflecting on *your* question and answering it.

Or the coachee might say, 'Do you mean X or Y?', not remembering that you won't answer any questions. Either shrug or just say, 'Yes!' Now, that may sound unhelpful, but you're indicating that it's the coachee's choice whether the questions mean X or Y. And when he chooses, he'll usually find a useful answer.

As a coach you create the space for people to think their own thoughts, and discover and surprise themselves with their wisdom. It is for this reason that you don't respond in a 'helpful' manner. As a result, you don't influence your coachees. That's how the Five-Minute Coach process stays 'clean'. (For more on Grove's Clean Language see the Introduction.)

Five-Minute tips

1   Although it may be tempting to use a phrase, and odd to pick just one word, you'll find asking about only *one* word is often more helpful to the coachee.

2   If you aren't sure which word to select, plump for a feeling, metaphor or verb (action word).

3   Repeat some of the coachee's words at the start of each question: 'And when ... what kind of ...?'

4   Ask the four core questions in the sequence given.

5   Write down the final outcome, repeating it out loud as you do so.

Five-Minute practice

Practise using the 'What kind of ...?' and 'And is there anything else about ...?' questions outside of coaching whenever you find an opportunity. Of course, ensure you use the other person's words when you ask the questions.

Make sure you use them at least once a day, at work or outside. You may want to find out more information for yourself, or to support someone else to think through and communicate their ideas more clearly.

Practise this activity until you find yourself asking the questions without even realising you are doing so – until after it's happened!

 ## Five-Minute story

Yvette is a specialist researcher and very well respected in her organisation. She asked Lynne for coaching as she had a strong desire to improve her work–life balance. Yvette was working longer and longer hours, including answering emails at weekends. She was exhausted.

One of the biggest problems Yvette experienced was the number of requests for help she was getting from colleagues across the organisation. Her reputation increased as various departments found her input really valuable. But work demands were becoming overwhelming.

Yvette really wanted to learn the skill of saying 'no', when appropriate. Lynne, making no comment or suggestions about how this intelligent and accomplished individual was perfectly capable of using the word 'no', took her through the Stage 3 questions in the Five-Minute Coach.

First, Yvette identified the attributes of 'no'. It had to be a polite and empathic 'no'. She could, of course, say 'no' sometimes. Yet it was important to her that she didn't develop a reputation for being unhelpful.

Then Yvette answered location questions about 'no' – it was 'inside me'. Her response to the whereabouts question was: 'It's right here' (pointing to her diaphragm). She continued: 'And – oh, that's interesting – it feels OK if I say "no" from here.'

When asked the final Stage 3 question, about what Yvette would like to have happen given all that she *now* knew, her response was quite clear. She wanted to feel OK about saying 'no' when she needed to. Only that wasn't all she said! Yvette followed with: 'And I *can!* I just have to say "no" from right here. That's easy now!' She was pointing to her diaphragm animatedly, whilst grinning widely.

Yvette didn't want an action plan. She had her action and was ready to make the change she wanted. She just had to 'say "no" from right here'. Lynne didn't completely understand what had happened for Yvette, as so often is the case with the Five-Minute Coach. But the coachee was fired up with a strategy that made perfect sense to her and was ready to create the change that she wanted.

 ## Five-Minute **practice**

Some people find it hard to ask the 'where' and 'whereabouts' questions when using the Five-Minute Coach. So finding opportunities to practise is really valuable. Just like the other two core questions in Stage 3, these questions glean useful information.

Find an opportunity to ask the 'where' and 'whereabouts' questions at least once a day for the next two weeks. When you put your mind to it, you'll be amazed *where* you can use them. For instance, let's say you get some feedback from your line manager. She says she'd like to see improvements in your figures. You can ask, 'Where in my figures?' and then ask a whereabouts question based on her response – all to get highly specific information. Although you may be able to access this information with a different question, your purpose, for now, is to get really familiar with using the location questions.

Five-Minute Coach Framework so far

Stage	Purpose	Questions
1	Identifying an outcome	**And what would you like to have happen?**
2	Choosing the best outcome	**And when** [outcome in coachee's words], *then* **what happens?** **And when** [last answer], *then* **what happens?** (Repeat question, with each answer, until no new answers emerge) **And** [outcome] **and** [recap all answers], **what are you drawn to most?**
3	Discovering more about the outcome	**And when** [new outcome], **what kind of** [word or phrase from outcome]**?** **And when** [last answer], **is there anything else about** [same word or phrase]**?** **And when** [last answer], **where is/are** [same word or phrase]**?** **And when** [last answer], **whereabouts** [last answer]**?** **And** [last answer]. **Given what you** *now* **know, what would you like to have happen?**

Five-Minute **conversations**

The four core Five-Minute Coach questions from Stage 3 are very effective information gatherers in any situation. In just five minutes or less, you can use these questions to great effect, improving effectiveness and efficiency. Some of the ways in which they have been used include:

- **Checking out joint understanding.** When agreements are made in meetings – for example, a list of actions to be undertaken – then asking questions of key words in each action description results in a better understanding of what everyone has agreed to. If words like 'review' or 'communication' are used, ask 'What kind of review?' and 'What kind of communication?' to generate more specific information for discussion and agreement.

- **Undertaking research.** The Stage 3 questions offer an invaluable and straightforward route to fact-finding. Use these questions in any situation wherever clarity of information will help you do a better job.

- **Requesting specific feedback.** Acquiring detailed, useful feedback can be a challenge. At work, for example, you may hear your boss tell you he'd like you to be more proactive. Rather than wonder what he means or make assumptions, you could ask 'What kind of proactive?' and 'Where?' You'll discover much more about what behavioural changes he is looking for and in what contexts.

- **Eliminating assumptions.** It's a natural human function to make our own meaning of what others say, which involves making assumptions. In many situations this is fine. However, when you find yourself in circumstances where it's important to have accurate information then use these Five-Minute Coach questions to find out more.

- **Handling disagreements.** When you find yourself disagreeing strongly with someone's opinion or suggestion, rather than fight harder to defend your position, ask questions! By getting a richer understanding of the other person's opinion you may identify a route to compromise or agreement that you hadn't anticipated. Alternatively, the new information might help you change your mind or tailor your argument specifically at the point you don't like.

- **Encouraging contribution.** When you are dealing with a quiet or shy person, he may be reluctant to discuss his opinions at length. The questions help you gently elicit the contribution of reluctant talkers who may well have a huge amount to offer.

- **Recovering a forgotten point or the original objectives of a discussion.** In animated discussions with enthusiastic contributors, an important or relevant point can be made that gets lost in the melee. Similarly, key objectives or agenda points can vanish as discussions go off on a tangent. Just a very simple question: 'And where is [good point or original objective]?' immediately brings it back into focus.

- **Building better relationships.** Asking the Stage 3 questions in any kind of general conversation demonstrates a level of curiosity about, and interest in, other people. This is a great way to build rapport, get someone talking and get to know them better.

Chapter 6
The Five-Minute Coach Stage 4

Action Planning

"It was all about me and reliant on me. The coach didn't help or collude, so I had to be my own champion. That was really great – I drew on reserves of courage, inspiration and inner strength that I don't always remember I have as people are always there to help and suggest things."

Stage 4: Action planning	**And what needs to happen for** [final outcome]**?**
	And is there anything else that needs to happen for [final outcome]**?** (Repeat question until you hear first 'no')
	And [final outcome and recap every action point]**, and is there anything else that needs to happen for** [final outcome]**?** (Repeat question until you hear second 'no')
	And [final outcome and recap every action point]**, and what needs to happen first?**
	And can [previous answer]**?**

Five-Minute **Stage 4** in brief

Now it's time to support your coachee to create a valuable action plan to help her achieve what she wants. You start with the latest – and final – outcome that your coachee identified in Stage 3.

One simple question starts the process:

> **And what needs to happen for** [final outcome]**?**

Write down the answer and then ask:

> **And is there anything else that needs to happen for** [final outcome]**?**

Ask this question repeatedly, writing down each answer carefully. Ask the same question again and again until you hear a 'no'. At this point, ask:

> **And** [final outcome and recap every action point], **and is there anything else that needs to happen for** [final outcome]**?**

It's likely the coachee will have a further action point. Write that down and ask again:

> **And is there anything else that needs to happen for** [final outcome]**?**

Keep on asking, and writing down the answers accurately, until you hear 'no' for the second time.

Now that an action plan exists, you help the coachee decide where to start by repeating each answer you logged, and asking your next question:

And [final outcome and recap every action point], **and what needs to happen first?**

When you have an answer, there's just one final question:

Can [previous answer]**?**

Once you have a firm 'yes', your coachee has a clear direction and path to follow. To make achieving her outcome even more likely, you move into the fifth and final stage of the Five-Minute Coach.

Example: Starting with a Stage 3 outcome

Coachee: To be more assertive!

Coach: **And what needs to happen for** you to be more assertive**?**

Coachee: I need to feel more confident.

Coach: **And is there anything else that needs to happen for** you to be more assertive**?**

Coachee: I need to remember I *do* know what I am talking about.

Coach: **And is there anything else that needs to happen for** you to be more assertive**?**

Coachee: I need to practise.

Coach: **And is there anything else that needs to happen for** you to be more assertive**?**

Coachee: No!

Coach: **And** to be more assertive, you need to feel more confident, to remember you *do* know what you're talking about, to practise. **And is there anything else that needs to happen for** you to be more assertive?

Coachee: I suppose … I could pick one person to try it out on.

Coach: **And is there anything else that needs to happen for** you to be more assertive?

Coachee: I need to test it gradually to make sure I am not coming across as aggressive.

Coach: **And is there anything else that needs to happen for** you to be more assertive?

Coachee: I could ask Jay for feedback. He shares my office and he'll tell me how he thinks I'm doing.

Coach: **And is there anything else that needs to happen for** you to be more assertive?

Coachee: No!

Coach: **And** to be more assertive, you need to feel more confident, to remember you *do* know what you're talking about, to practise, pick one person to try it out on, test it gradually to make sure you are not coming across as aggressive, ask Jay for feedback. **And what needs to happen first?**

Coachee: I need to remember I *do* know what I'm talking about.

Coach: **And can** you remember you *do* know what you're talking about?

Coachee: Yes!

Discovering Stage 4

You've helped your coachee to create a well-defined outcome as you moved through the previous three stages of the Five-Minute Coach. However, a clear goal is often not enough to create change. There needs to be action. Stage 4 invites the coachee to produce a detailed plan for what needs to happen next.

The role of planning

Producing detailed, step-by-step action plans to implement complex projects and meet major goals is a commonplace approach. Plans for business, projects, operations, service, marketing and more are created and used in organisations large and small. Many of us are less likely to put together similar plans for achieving smaller scale personal goals – and then we are disappointed when we don't *achieve* these goals.

Coaching often puts a spotlight on making action plans for individuals to help them to make things happen. The Five-Minute Coach is no exception and includes a useful process for finding out not only what needs to be done, but whether the coachee is capable of initiating the action.

Your coachee has an outcome or objective that – providing she's been through the earlier stages of the Five-Minute Coach – she knows a lot about and is quite committed to achieving. If you're someone who's motivated by *doing* things, you'll no doubt be pleased to move into the action planning stage, after putting so much attention on pursuing the best possible outcome for the coachee.

Creating a powerful action plan

Yet again, this stage of the Five-Minute Coach is carefully structured and works when you follow the procedure. One of the questions is asked over and over again, which may challenge you as coach but is very helpful to the coachee.

Start with the coachee's final outcome, derived from Stage 3, and ask the first action planning question, inserting the outcome, no matter how long it is:

And what needs to happen for [final outcome]**?**

Having accurately written down the answer, ask your next question:

And is there anything else that needs to happen for [final outcome]**?**

For example:

I want to have more influence on the marketing campaign.

And what needs to happen for you to have more influence on the marketing campaign**?**

Notice how, once more, you lose the 'want' and phrase your question to imply the coachee's final outcome is possible. In addition, observe that the wording of your question is not: 'And what do *you need to do*?' Instead, 'And what needs to happen ...' is less burdensome for the coachee, and stimulates more creative thinking around the issue. As you come to the end of this stage, you check in with your coachee that the first task is possible – as far as she's concerned. You'll read about that a little later.

This is the only stage in the Five-Minute Coach framework when you don't repeat the last answer before asking your next question. Instead, your repetition happens at two summary points during this stage.

Once you've noted down your coachee's answer, continue to ask the same question repeatedly. You may notice the coachee seems to have the action points in an illogical order. That's fine – the process deals with this later.

You may be tempted to stop after a few iterations, thinking that the same question multiple times will irritate the other person. Don't stop! Keep going until you hear the first 'no' in response to your question. Then, you lead up to asking again by repeating, carefully, all of the action points in turn and then asking if there is anything else that needs to happen to achieve the outcome:

> **And** [final outcome and recap every action point], **and is there anything *else* that need to happen for** [final outcome]**?**

Our example might continue like this:

> **And** you want to have more influence on the marketing campaign, you need to meet with the brand manager, attend marketing briefing meetings, write a paper for the communications team. **And is there anything else that needs to happen for** you to have more influence on the marketing campaign**?**

Odd though it may seem to ask this question when you've already heard that there is nothing else, the coachee will usually give you another answer. By recapping the outcome and all the action points you create the environment in which she hears all her answers at once, and often other things that she'd not previously been aware of pop into her mind. So, using our example, you might hear from the coachee:

> Oh yes, I need to make the time to get involved with marketing.

In response, you continue to ask the original 'anything else' question until you get to a resounding 'no'. In the example, this might go something like:

Coach: **And is there anything *else* that needs to happen for** you to have more influence on the marketing campaign**?**

Coachee: I need to get the new business project signed off and out of the way.

Coach: **And is there anything *else* that needs to happen for** you to have more influence on the marketing campaign**?**

Coachee: No.

Now that your coachee has said 'no' a second time, move onto the next question in this stage:

> **And** [final outcome and recap every action point], **and what needs to happen *first*?**

At last you've reached the final question in Stage 4 when you ask about the answer to the previous question:

> **And can** [answer to previous question]**?**

So in our example, these two last enquiries by the coach, with the coachee's response, might sound something like:

Coach: **And** you want to have more influence on the marketing campaign, you need to meet with the brand manager, attend marketing briefing meetings, write a paper for the communications team, make the time to get involved with marketing, get the new business project signed off and out of the way. **And what needs to happen first?**

Coachee: I need to write a paper for the communications team.

Coach: **And can** you write a paper for the communications team**?**

Coachee: Yes.

Listen carefully to your coachee's answer to this question. Is it a convincing 'yes'? If the voice suggests more of a 'maybe' than a 'yes', or you hear a 'probably' or 'I think so', head to the troubleshooting section later in this chapter.

When you have a believable 'yes', you've finished this stage and are ready to move on to Stage 5. Remember that *you* don't need to be convinced that your coachee can do what *she* thinks she can. You accept what she says. As long as the coachee is convinced, it's possible the first thing in the action plan will happen. If she can't make that first step happen she'll discover that herself soon enough, and then she may be back to you for more coaching.

Figure 7 outlines the steps in Stage 4. You'll notice that at the end, should your coachee decide that the first thing identified *can't* be done, there is another process to go through. (To find out more about this, go to the Five-Minute troubleshooting section later in this chapter.)

Working on the action plan

You may have noticed that during the action planning process you only ask someone to prioritise the first action point. Normal planning protocols would say that you sort an entire action plan into order, one step at a time, probably review timescales, add deadlines and more.

The Five-Minute Coach doesn't do this for one very good reason: most coachees don't *need* to work out that much detail for their plan. Once they are motivated to get going (more about that in Stage 5) and know the first thing that needs to be done, they start making progress towards their outcomes. The unconscious mind, as well as the conscious mind, is now primed to achieve what the coachee wants. For those who prefer to put more structure into their action plan, well, once they've been through the Five-Minute Coach they'll be keen to do that for themselves.

People are often surprised to find that having tackled the first thing, many of the other actions identified don't even need to be done. Yes, things change and people find themselves achieving their outcome in ways they hadn't known were possible. For example, think about a time you prepared for a difficult conversation. You may have had a clear outcome, worked out all the things you wanted to say and what to say first. After you said that first thing, a conversation ensued that you certainly didn't predict. You responded to what the other person said, and the conversation took a very different direction – yet you still met your outcome.

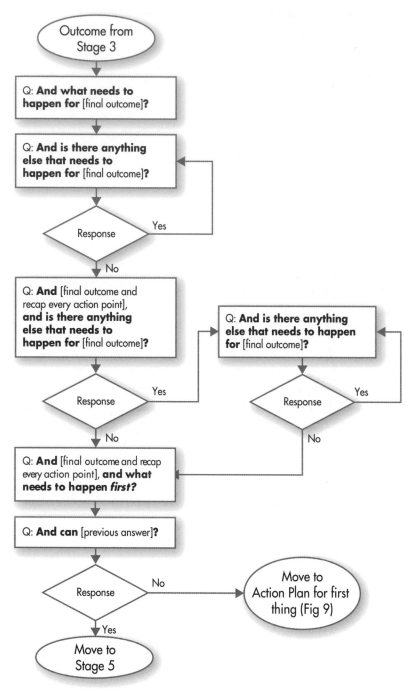

Figure 7: The Stage 4 Five-Minute Coach process

One more factor may sometimes surprise you during this final part of the action planning stage. Having listed all that needs to happen to achieve an outcome, you may hear about a first action that the coachee hadn't mentioned before. Just write down her answer and continue to ask the next question: 'And can [previous answer]?'

Remember

You're coaching, rather than advising or suggesting possible actions or ways your coachee might get what she wants. You ask questions to assist her to think through her action plan – which may be quite different from the action plan *you'd* have created if *you* were trying to get where your coachee wants to be. Resist the temptation to make a few suggestions as to what she might do, or what she might tackle first, however blindingly obvious those things might seem to you.

Really useful questions

The Stage 4 Five-Minute Coach questions put attention on what needs to happen to get anything done. Used conversationally, they quickly focus people's thinking and help them to move out of stuck situations. The identification of what needs to happen first, and whether the person can take that first step, generally removes the need for a sequential action plan with timescales. This can be quite liberating, removing a part of the planning process which can itself become a blockage to getting started.

 ## Five-Minute **example**

In Stage 3, Chris discovered more about his outcome and concluded that what he really wanted was to find it easy to meet his deadlines. Amira now leads Chris through the Five-Minute Coach action planning questions.

Amira: **And what needs to happen for** you to find it easy to meet your deadlines**?**

Chris: I need to set time aside to go through all the information on my desk and computer so that I can determine my priorities.

Amira: **And is there anything *else* that needs to happen for** you to find it easy to meet your deadlines**?**

Chris: I need to look at what's urgent, and what's important.

Amira: **And is there anything *else* that needs to happen for** you to find it easy to meet your deadlines**?**

Chris: I need to check in with you as to what you think is most important.

Amira: **And is there anything *else* that needs to happen for** you to find it easy to meet your deadlines**?**

Chris: I need to show you my list of priorities and make sure it's agreed.

Amira: **And is there anything *else* that needs to happen for** you to find it easy to meet your deadlines**?**

Chris: I need to get rid of some things ... pass other things on to Alex.

Amira: **And is there anything *else* that needs to happen for** you to find it easy to meet your deadlines**?**

Chris: No.

Amira: **And** to find it easy to meet your deadlines, you need to set time aside to go through all the information on your desk and computer so that you can determine your priorities ... look at what's urgent and what's important ... check in with me as to what I think is important ... show me your list of priorities and make sure it's agreed ... get rid of some things, pass other things on to Alex. **And is there anything *else* that needs to happen for** you to find it easy to meet your deadlines**?**

Chris: I need to make sure that I know which pieces of work will make most impact, you know, make a difference.

Amira: **And is there anything *else* that needs to happen for** you to find it easy to meet your deadlines?

Chris: I need to block some time out in my diary for each of my priorities.

Amira: **And is there anything *else* that needs to happen for** you to find it easy to meet your deadlines?

Chris: I need to set some mini targets – stepping stones – to ensure that each deadline is on target for being met.

Amira: **And is there anything *else* that needs to happen for** you to find it easy to meet all your deadlines?

Chris: No.

Amira: **And** to find it easy to meet your deadlines, you need to set time aside to go through all the information on your desk and computer so that you can determine your priorities ... look at what's urgent and what's important ... check in with me as to what I think is important ... show me your list of priorities and make sure it's agreed ... get rid of some things, pass other things on to Alex ... make sure you know which pieces of work will make a difference ... block some time out in your diary for each of your priorities ... set some mini targets – stepping stones – to ensure that each deadline is on target for being met. **And what needs to happen first?**

Chris: I need to set time aside and go through the information on my desk and computer, so I can begin to prioritise.

Amira: **And can** you set time aside and go through the information on your desk and computer, and begin to prioritise?

Chris: Yes!

Chris is smiling and gives a small nod as he says he can take his first step. His voice is quite emphatic, so Amira believes he's ready for the final piece of coaching in Stage 5.

	2 find it easy 2 mt my deadlines
WNH	Set time aside 2 go thru all info on desk on + computer so can determine priorities
AE	Look at what's urgent + what's imp
AE	Check in with u, what think's most imp.
AE	Show u my list priorities + make sure agreed
AE	Get rid some things, pass others ≫ Alex
AE	No
AE	Make sure know which pieces wk will make most impact/difference
AE	Block some time out, in diary, 4 each of priorities
AE	Set some mini-tgts, steppg stones 2 ensure each ddline on tgt4 being met
AE	—
1st	Set time aside + go thru info on desk + compr so can begin 2 prioritise
Can	Yes

Figure 8: Amira's handwritten notes of Stage 4 coaching session

Five-Minute troubleshooting

On a rare occasion, you may ask the very last question of Stage 4, to check out if the first action point can happen, and find the answer is 'no' – or the coachee may say 'yes' but in a hesitant or unconvincing way.

Should this happen you need to do an additional piece of coaching. Your coachee requires another action plan – one for that first thing that needs to happen. If you don't both have the time right now, you may need to suggest:

> You need a first thing you *can* do. Since we don't have time now, shall we schedule in some time soon?

If you *do* have the time to continue, or when you resume, your next question is:

> **And what needs to happen for**
> [first thing coachee said needed to happen]**?**

Then continue through all the Five-Minute Coach Stage 4 questions again, asking each question about the first thing that needs to happen.

As an example, let's look at what Amira would have done if Chris had said 'no' or a hesitant 'yes'.

Amira: **And can** you set time aside and go through the information on your desk and computer, and begin to prioritise**?**

Chris: I'm not sure ... hmm ... maybe.

Amira: **And what needs to happen for** you to set time aside and go through the information on your desk and computer, and begin to prioritise**?**

And then Amira continues into this second action planning session.

Only once have we experienced facilitating three action plans before hearing a confident 'Yes!' from the coachee. Surprisingly, it didn't take very long. The coachee thought it was a great coaching session because she walked away knowing exactly what to do next.

If this happens to you, act as if second and even third action plans are completely normal. Your reaction will reassure your coachee and help her to overcome any blockages to getting started.

Figure 9 outlines how to go through the action plan process when your coachee has decided he can't make his first action point

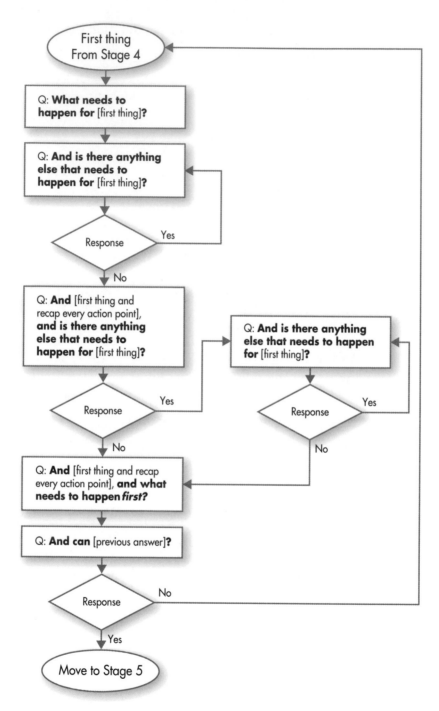

Figure 9: The action plan for 'first thing' process

happen. You'll notice it's very similar to coaching to achieve a final outcome (Figure 7), replacing the final outcome with the first thing that needs to happen.

 ## Five-Minute **tips**

1   If your coachee's outcome is very long, don't attempt to shorten it. It may seem long-winded, but use the precise words each time you ask the action planning questions.

2   Be relaxed about the repetitive nature of the questions. It's fine for the coachee! Those who like detailed action plans need you to ask the action planning questions many times. Those who prefer broad brush planning will give you both 'no's quite quickly.

3   If you hear a 'no' answer, make sure it's a firm and decisive 'no' by keeping silent for a few seconds. If the 'no' was a reflex response, the coachee often adds to the answer after a little more thinking time. When you resist filling the space with your next question, more information is likely to emerge.

4   After your coachee gives you her first decisive 'no', recap the outcome and action points to date and ask your next question, emphasising 'anything', rather than 'else': 'And is there *anything* else that needs to happen for [final outcome]?'

5   When you hear a 'yes' to the very final question of this stage, make sure it's a firm and decisive 'yes', not a 'maybe', 'possibly' or 'I think so'.

Five-Minute **practice**

Think of something you want to achieve but haven't yet made much progress on. Take the questions from this stage of the Five-Minute Coach and run yourself through the process. Keep on asking yourself the questions. Write down each answer as you go. Then notice how the process has helped you organise your thoughts and get started.

Five-Minute **story**

We used the Five-Minute Coach to work with a team responsible for introducing a significant culture change programme into the organisation. We took all eight members of the team through the first three stages of the Five-Minute Coach to develop – and agree – their team outcome: to gain fast and positive buy-in to the change initiative.

We then worked through the action planning process with team members. They each contributed a range of action points that they identified needed to happen to achieve the outcome. Everything was recorded on flip charts as each idea was added, and they quickly chose and agreed the first thing that needed to happen. As a group, they then restructured the action plan, allocating timings and individual responsibilities. They went away well-motivated to get started.

Six months later Mariette checked in with the leader, John. She asked how his team had progressed with the action plan and what the results had been. John looked down and confessed: 'We haven't looked at the action plan in months. You know how it is, we got busy, the plan got put in the drawer and it just didn't happen. Things are going *really* well though. We are exceeding expectations on employee engagement with the change initiative.'

Mariette was curious, so enquired further. When she reviewed the action plan with John, he noticed that the first thing on the plan had been done – and quite quickly. Much to his surprise, a number of the other action points had been implemented too. He'd just forgotten they were in the plan! And a number of tasks hadn't been completed as it had turned out they weren't necessary for the result they wanted – and got.

 # Five-Minute practice

Next time you are at a meeting with at least three people in it, use the Five-Minute Coach action planning questions to create a plan for something that needs to be done. You may want to tell your colleagues that you'd like to use a new process to draw out the action plan, with their permission. Explain that they'll each get a turn, and they can't challenge anyone else's contribution, or discuss any item, until the process is complete. Decide who will answer the question first. If you have a flip chart, record the meeting objective or subject at the top, followed by answers as they're given.

For example, at the top of the flip chart could be a goal: 'Cover Isabella's maternity leave'. You know your first question: 'And what needs to happen to cover Isabella's maternity leave?'

Take a turn to answer the question yourself, if appropriate. When you get a 'no', recap all the action points before asking the next person the question. Keep asking each person in turn until you reach the point where everyone has said 'no'. Wait for this to happen because it's possible that one person's answer may get another person thinking. Repeat back the list of action points you have gathered, and ask the group, 'And what needs to happen first?' When they've agreed, check whether that thing can happen.

Notice what different results you get using this process, during which people don't need to fight for air time and contributors' ideas stimulate more ideas.

Five-Minute Coach Framework so far

Stage	Purpose	Questions
1	Identifying an outcome	**And what would you like to have happen?**
2	Choosing the best outcome	**And when** [outcome in coachee's words], ***then* what happens?** **And when** [last answer], ***then* what happens?** (Repeat question, with each answer, until no new answers emerge) **And** [outcome] **and** [recap all answers], **what are you drawn to most?**
3	Discovering more about the outcome	**And when** [new outcome], **what kind of** [word or phrase from outcome]**?** **And when** [last answer], **is there anything else about** [same word or phrase]**?** **And when** [last answer], **where is/are** [same word or phrase]**?** **And when** [last answer], **whereabouts** [last answer]**?** **And** [last answer]. **Given what you *now* know, what would you like to have happen?**

Stage	Purpose	Questions
4	Action planning	**And what needs to happen for** [final outcome]**?**
		And is there anything else that needs to happen for [final outcome]**?** (Repeat question until you hear first 'no')
		And [final outcome and recap every action point], **and is there anything else that needs to happen for** [final outcome]**?** (Repeat question until you hear second 'no')
		And [final outcome and recap every action point], **and what needs to happen *first*?**
		And can [previous answer]**?**

Five-Minute **conversations**

This part of the Five-Minute Coach offers a highly practical approach to planning, quickly and effectively, in many different contexts. It works with teams and groups of people as well as with individuals. Here are some applications:

● **Resisting taking on other's problems**. When you hear people's problems, or what they want to achieve, in conversation, it's easy to get drawn in. You may find yourself offering solutions, advice or opinions – or even offering to fix things. Some time later you can find that you're so busy working on other people's issues that you lose sight of your own priorities. 'And what needs to happen?' is an unassuming question which helps other people whilst keeping ownership of matters where it belongs – with them.

- **Moving someone from complaint to action.** Next time you hear something like, 'I really wish this place was more organised', ask the question: 'And what needs to happen for this place to be more organised?' Immediately you lead that person to start thinking differently and take some responsibility for making something happen.

- **Developing joint action plans for groups and teams.** Not only is this process a great way of generating a shared team action plan, but the team members buy in jointly to taking responsibility for making something happen. This leads to much better team working and improved performance.

- **Reducing overwhelm and stress**. When you come across people who have so much happening that they just doesn't know where to put their attention, Stage 4 can make all the difference. Asking these simple questions quickly identifies what they need to do, so they can prioritise and start to make progress.

- **Project planning.** Identify the different things that need to happen to bring about a project with the Five-Minute Coach, systematically work out the detail and map out a specific plan.

- **Creating personal action plans.** When you find yourself with objectives, projects and even fairly simple tasks that just aren't getting done, take a few minutes to ask yourself the Stage 4 questions. You quickly create meaningful and useful plans, and that all-important first step to get started.

- **Making goals achievable.** For people with big goals, complex tasks and long-term projects, a Five-Minute Coach action plan enables them to identify actions without putting pressure on themselves. They may discover that they don't have to do everything and others could contribute to making the outcome happen.

Motivating to Act

"The coaching allowed me to realise and remember my own potential and that I have freedom to make decisions about my own life without waiting for someone to tell me how to do it. I was pleasantly surprised, with a plan for the future by the end - all from my own head!"

Stage 5: Motivate to act	**And when** [first thing], ***then* what happens?** (Repeat until coachee is in a positive state and seems keen to act)
	And is that a good place to stop? (Hand over notes)

Five-Minute Stage 5 in brief

Now that your coachee has an outcome and a plan of how to achieve it, your purpose in this final stage of the Five-Minute Coach is to leave her feeling impelled to take action. You use a question you've practised in Stage 2 to help her get a sense of how good things will be as the future unfolds and the outcome is achieved.

Using your coachee's words for the first thing that needs to happen (change the tense if necessary), ask:

And when [first thing], ***then* what happens?**

Having completed Stage 2, you've probably anticipated that you repeat this question with your coachee's latest answer:

And when [answer to last question], ***then* what happens?**

Ask your question with enthusiasm and use encouraging noises to assist the coachee to feel the beneficial effects of each consequence as it emerges. Notice the effect this final piece of questioning is having on her. Keep asking the same question until you see or hear some positive emotion. For example, she may be speaking enthusiastically, smiling, nodding or changing posture. Now your coachee has engaged more fully with the whole outcome and action plan. She's motivated and energised to get started.

All that's left to do is to check the coachee is happy to end the coaching. Your final question is:

And is that a good place to stop?

As she agrees, hand over the notes you've taken.

Example: Starting with Stage 4 first step

Coach: **And when** you read the book, ***then* what happens?**

Coachee: I remind myself of what I need to do, and I get re-enthused about doing it.

Coach: **And when** you remind yourself, and you get re-enthused, ***then* what happens?**

Coachee: I find myself making the changes, without even trying.

Coach: **And when** you find yourself making the changes, without even trying, **_then_ what happens?**

Coachee: Then life is easy, and I'm becoming my best without effort (smiling).

Coach: **And is that a good place to stop?**

Coachee: Yes!

Discovering Stage 5

This is the final stage of the Five-Minute Coach, where you make sure that your coachee will start to work towards achieving his outcome. Your role in this part of the coaching is to ensure that as well as having a plan in mind, or on paper, the coachee *feels* motivated and enthused to make things happen.

The difference that makes the difference

Having coached someone through three stages of developing an outcome – what he wants – and supported him to work through a comprehensive action plan, you could be forgiven for thinking that's enough. And in some cases you'd be right. Your coachee could be chomping at the bit to get started.

However, we have ourselves coached people to identify an outcome and work out exactly what to do to achieve it, only to find at the next meeting that the coachee hasn't actually done *anything*. Of course there's usually a rationale – 'I've just been too busy' being one of the most common.

We've put the final stage of the Five-Minute Coach together to overcome the problem of people not getting started on their action plans. With Stage 5, any resistance or reticence to take the first step of the action plan soon fades away.

Stimulating action

You're already familiar with the question in this stage. You used it in Stage 2 to explore the consequences of achieving an outcome:

And when ... *then* **what happens?**

In this last stage of coaching, you ask the question not about the outcome, but about the *action* that your coachee identified as the first thing that needs to happen:

And when [first thing], *then* **what happens?**

As you have been doing to date, write down key words and phrases from your coachee's response. Use these to ask the question again:

And when [answer to last question], *then* **what happens?**

You probably know by now that you are going to ask this question multiple times, using the coachee's previous answer on each occasion. You're engaging the coachee, step by step, with the process of moving towards his outcome. You lead him to rehearse the route to success in his mind, in the same way that top athletes prepare to win a competition. Your coachee ends up in a very positive state and inspired to take action.

Once you're sure that your coachee is enthused, positive and ready to act, it's time to conclude the coaching. Do this by checking in with the simple question:

And is that a good place to stop?

In our experience the coachee will be ready to stop at this point and say 'yes'. Then offer the notes that you've taken of the coaching session. In the unlikely event that he *doesn't* want to stop, you ask the very first question again: 'And what would you like to have happen?' If the coachee's response is another problem or outcome to explore, check whether it's appropriate to do that now, and if not, book another meeting.

Figure 10 outlines the steps to follow in Stage 5.

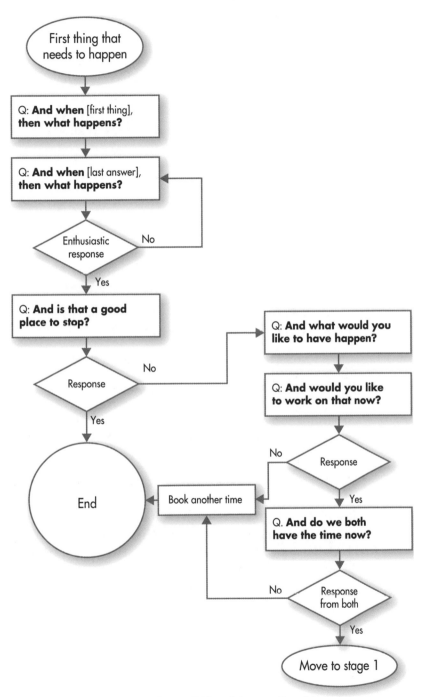

Figure 10: The Stage 5 Five-Minute Coach process

Encouraging all the way

To help get your coachee ready to take action, use your voice, encouraging noises and facial expressions to add emphasis to some of the positives. Even when you're not giving much eye contact, a coachee will hear encouragement and enthusiasm in your voice. And slowing down positive phrases gives words emphasis and allows them time to sink in.

For example, Tyrrell is coaching Ruth. The first step, from her action plan, is to book a meeting with David.

Tyrrell: **And when** you book a meeting with David, ***then* what happens?**

Ruth: Then we can create a plan to work together to solve the invoicing problem.

Tyrrell: **And when** you create a plan to solve the invoicing problems, ***then* what happens?**

Ruth: Then I won't have frustrated customers and they will place more orders.

Tyrrell: Hmm (Tyrrell nods). **And when** you *don't* have frustrated customers and (next words said slowly) they place *more* orders, ***then* what happens?**

Ruth: I meet all my targets and am *very* happy! (Ruth sits back in her chair and laughs)

Notice that, as in Stage 2, Tyrrell changes Ruth's words to the present tense, so she has the experience of hearing her thoughts as if they were a reality right now. He makes an encouraging noise, 'Hmm', whilst nodding, uses his voice to emphasise and adds enthusiasm to his repetition of the words that sound positive. Tyrrell even slows down a key phrase. As a result, Ruth feels in such an upbeat mood that she laughs.

Remember

In this final stage of the Five-Minute Coach your role becomes more encouraging. You may or may not believe that things will pan out as your coachee suggests. Either way, refrain from commenting. Just ask your questions, with a positive emphasis and warmth, and be as upbeat as your coachee is as he identifies even more positive outputs from achieving his outcome.

Really useful questions

Of course, like each of the other aspects of the Five-Minute Coach, this part of the framework also provides a very good stand-alone technique for motivating others. People often don't get around to doing things that seem small, insignificant or plain difficult. They can easily overlook the fact that it is these things which could lead to a much bigger, long-term gain. By connecting them with that bigger picture, the motivation is far more easily found to get started, and procrastination can be wiped away in an instant.

Five-Minute example

Amira and Chris have worked their way through Chris's action plan, as you read in the previous chapter. Chris identified the first thing that he needed to do, and he confirmed to Amira that he could do it. You remember that the first thing that needed to happen was for Chris to 'set time aside and go through the information on my desk and computer, so I can begin to prioritise'.

Amira: **And when** you set time aside and go through the information on your desk and computer, and begin to prioritise, **_then_ what happens?**

Chris: Then I can check in with you and agree the priorities.

Amira: **And when** you check in with me and agree the priorities, **_then_ what happens?**

Chris: Then I'll block time in my diary to tackle each piece of work.

Amira: **And when** you block time in your diary to tackle each piece of work, *then* **what happens?**

Chris: Then I achieve the deadlines.

Amira: Hmm (nodding). **And when** you *achieve* the deadlines, *then* **what happens?**

Chris: Then I feel great – and others will notice I'm on top of things too.

Amira: **And when** you feel *great* – and (next words said slowly) others will notice you're on top of things too, *then* **what happens?**

Chris: Then I'll be better placed to move up to a bigger job (big smile on face).

Amira: **And** (big smile on face too) **is that a good place to stop?**

Chris: Yes!

Amira: (Hands over notes) Thank you. And if you'd like to let me know how you get on, then please do.

Amira has taken Chris through the questioning until Chris has become enthused. She helped by slowing down an important phrase and emphasising a key word, 'great'. He's worked out he can get what he wants and Amira can see from Chris's smile that he is now feeling positive. Chris is ready to act.

can	Yes
—	
TWH	Check in with u + agree priorities
TWH	Block time in diary to tackle each pce wk
TWH	Achieve deadlines
TWH	Feel great. Others know I'm on top of things
TWH	Better placed to ↑ to bigger job
Stop	Yes

Figure 11: Amira's handwritten notes of Stage 5 coaching session

 # Five-Minute **troubleshooting**

In Stage 5, as in other stages, you may find that when you start to repeat an answer you've been given, before you have a chance to ask a question, the coachee starts talking again. Challenging though this may feel, when you are trying to lead someone carefully through the procedure of the Five-Minute Coach, you can relax.

In fact, this is a really good reflection on how well you're coaching. You are achieving the key goal of aiding the coachee to think, and think more deeply, about the issue he is working on. By not bringing in any of your own words or opinions, and asking only the Five-Minute Coach questions, which are clean questions, you keep him totally focused on his own thoughts. More ideas are coming up for him even before you can ask your next question. This is especially true when you are asking a question repeatedly, so your coachee can begin to anticipate your question.

All you need to do is to let the coachee talk without interrupting. If you're looking at him, usually the coachee will make eye contact with you when he's ready. If you're in a formal coaching session, and writing notes rather than giving eye contact, you can allow a silence to develop before you repeat back some or all of his answer, and ask your question.

Five-Minute tips

1   Enhance your coachee's enthusiasm by adding emphasis to positive words and using encouraging noises and facial expressions.

2   Slow your pace when repeating positive phrases you've heard, allowing the coachee time to enjoy imagining that future achievement.

3   Ensure your voice reflects anticipation of a positive answer as you ask each question.

4   As you ask, 'And is this a good place to stop?', do so with an air of finality, giving your coachee a clear indication that the session has finished.

5   Now that you've reached the end of the coaching, say goodbye to your coachee and refrain from discussing or giving your opinion on anything from the session.

Five-Minute practice

You may have noticed that sometimes in conversation we communicate vocally but without actual words. You might say 'hmm' which, depending on the voice tone, might suggest you are accepting another's viewpoint, pausing to think or about to disagree. You may use 'uhuh', 'oh' or even utter a loud sigh. All these will be interpreted in different ways by the person you're communicating with, largely depending on your tone, facial expression and body language.

Practise using these non-verbal expressions in place of talking. Identify some interactions when you allow the other person to talk for several minutes whilst you say nothing. Instead, create an environment that allows someone to talk freely and without interruption, through your encouraging noises, smiles and nods. This is great practice for using the same techniques with the Five-Minute Coach.

Five-Minute story

Vea was feeling stuck. She'd been in the same role for a long time and had become bored. She wanted a new challenge – ideally a job which involved her learning new skills, whilst still using much of her experience in managing a clinical department. Vea raised her issue with Mariette in a coaching session.

Vea had an outcome. She wanted a new job. She had all the answers to the first four stages of the Five-Minute Coach as she'd thought it all through at length. She knew that her first action was to update her CV to fit the kind of positions that she was interested in. Yet she hadn't done it.

Reworking her CV needed to be done in Vea's own time, and she didn't have a lot of that. After all she was a busy manager with a young family. There were always other priorities. And the longer time went on without positive action, the more stressed Vea was becoming about her failure to make time to work through her CV.

Mariette took Vea through the final stage of the Five-Minute Coach to work through what happens once she's taken her first step. The answers were straightforward – after the CV was revised, Vea would apply for jobs. Over time she'd be invited to interviews. Ultimately she would be offered a new and better job.

Of course Vea already knew all of this. However, the big difference the Five-Minute Coach made was the impact it had on Vea's motivation. She got a taste of what it would be like to be in her new job and became excited about taking the first step. A few months later, having taken action, Vea was offered exactly the job she was looking for.

Five-Minute **practice**

Next time you hear somebody complaining that they never seem to get around to doing something, ask the question from this stage of the Five-Minute Coach: 'And when [you do that thing], *then* what happens?' If it seems useful, repeat the question several times, using the person's last answer in each case. Notice what emerges.

For some, you notice you've helped them find the motivation they need to do something. For others, it may well be that the consequences of taking that action are just not motivating enough to make it a worthwhile thing to do. At that point they can stop bemoaning the fact that they haven't started something and be content with the fact that it doesn't need doing.

And for further practice, pay attention to what you say – to others or yourself. What have you been putting off? Take yourself through the questions and discover what difference the new information makes.

Five-Minute Coach complete framework

Stage	Purpose	Questions
1	Identifying an outcome	**And what would you like to have happen?**
2	Choosing the best outcome	**And when** [outcome in coachee's words], ***then* what happens?** **And when** [last answer]**, then what happens?** (Repeat question, with each answer, until no new answers emerge) **And** [outcome] **and** [recap all answers]**, what are you drawn to most?**
3	Discovering more about the outcome	**And when** [new outcome]**, what kind of** [word or phrase from outcome]? **And when** [last answer]**, is there anything else about** [same word or phrase]? **And when** [last answer]**, where is/are** [same word or phrase]? **And when** [last answer]**, whereabouts** [last answer]? **And** [last answer]. **Given what you now know, what would you like to have happen?**

Stage	Purpose	Questions
4	Action planning	**And what needs to happen for** [final outcome]**?**
		And is there anything else that needs to happen for [final outcome]**?** (Repeat question until you hear first 'no')
		And [final outcome and recap every action point], **and is there anything else that needs to happen for** [final outcome]**?** (Repeat question until you hear second 'no')
		And [final outcome and recap every action point], **and what needs to happen first?**
		And can [previous answer]**?**
5	Motivate to act	**And when** [first thing], **_then_ what happens?** (Repeat until coachee is in a positive state and seems keen to act)
		And is that a good place to stop? (Hand over notes)

Five-Minute **conversations**

The Stage 5 Five-Minute Coach question has many uses in everyday conversations. In Chapter 4 we explored a number of ways to use its shortened version, 'And *then* what happens?' to look at consequences of particular outcomes or objectives.

Here are some examples of the question in use, outside of coaching, to motivate and enthuse.

- **Motivating others.** When people tell you about something they want in a lacklustre way, just ask, 'And when [you have outcome], *then* what happens?' When they explore the benefits of getting what they want, they are likely to become much more energised and proactive.

- **Overcoming procrastination**. People sometimes delay doing things they really need to do but don't *want* to do. Using this Five-Minute Coach question may help identify benefits to tackling something that they hadn't previously thought of, making them more inclined to start.

- **Resisting giving advice.** Often people like to unload, but are not really seeking advice or opinions from others. Asking this simple question helps another person to explore an issue more effectively and appreciate being listened to.

- **Resolving a dilemma.** When someone is stuck with a dilemma that makes it hard to choose what to do next, ask, 'And *then* what happens?' Ask the question repeatedly of each option. The person will have much more information with which to make a decision and move forward.

- **Making a goal achievable.** Some objectives, goals and dreams seem too big or far away to focus on. This very simple question changes the person's experience, making the goal seem much more manageable or closer. In turn, the goal appears more achievable and the person is enthused to get started.

Chapter 8

Dealing with the Unexpected

You've learned all about how the Five-Minute Coach works, how to use the questions and work with a coachee. You'll find that most coaching using the Five-Minute Coach goes smoothly and to plan. You ask the questions, coachees find great insights in their answers and go away focused and motivated to make things happen. However, infrequently – as with most things in life – you may just find things don't quite go to plan. Despite all your best efforts you get an unexpected response to a question you asked.

To help you deal with these unusual situations, and other things that you might have concerns about, we outline here how to handle the main issues that trainee Five-Minute Coaches have raised. You may wish to familiarise yourself with all the possible difficulties now or refer to them when you come across a sticky situation.

The most important thing to remember, should you find your Five-Minute Coaching session not going quite to plan, is to stay calm and look confident – even if you don't feel it. If you avoid getting into discussion and keep asking questions, you are likely to keep the coaching moving forward successfully.

If that doesn't work, then the strategies outlined in this chapter will equip you to deal with almost anything.

In the first section below, you'll find some issues that might occur at any stage of the coaching, and how to deal with them. After that you'll find a further five sections of FAQs covering specific queries which might come up at each particular stage of the Five-Minute Coach. Throughout you will find questions grouped under up to three headings:
(1) keeping ownership with the coachee,
(2) managing the process and
(3) managing yourself.

General troubleshooting FAQs

Keeping ownership with the coachee

1 *The coachee asks me for my opinion in the middle of the session. Do I reply?*

   No. This approach is based on you *not* influencing your coachee with your ideas and opinions. Shrug, limit your eye contact and keep silent for a little longer than you feel comfortable with. If the coachee still has not responded, then repeat the last answer, ignoring the request for your opinion, and ask your next question.

2 *After I ask a question the coachee asks me, 'What do you mean?' How do I respond?*

   As a Five-Minute Coach you never get into dialogue during a session. You've already said at the start that you will not answer questions once the session has started. So, hold fire, don't respond and wait. Most times the coachee finds an answer. If you've waited, without direct eye contact and in silence, for a couple of seconds and you feel uncomfortable, then slowly and deliberately repeat the question you just asked.

3 *The coachee keeps trying to engage me in conversation by making eye contact. What do I do?*

   Ask your question. Look away if you aren't already doing so and keep a neutral expression. The coachee may be looking at you to gauge whether you understand what she's saying. You know that your understanding of the content is not an important part of this coaching. So keep a poker face!

4 *The coachee gets emotional during the session. What do I do?*

   Sit quietly and wait. It's important not to be drawn into conversation about the emotion so avoid direct eye contact as much as possible. Count to 10, and if the coachee hasn't said anything further, ask, 'And what would you like to have happen?'

5   *The coachee says something that is patently untrue, such as 'senior managers care more about profits than staff'. How do I respond?*

Accept the statement at face value, even if you disagree. Continue with your questioning. In this case, since this is probably not something the coachee wants, you ask, 'And when senior management cares more about profits than staff, what would you like to have happen?'

Managing the process

6   *After I ask a question, there is a long silence and the coachee stares into the distance and doesn't speak. What should I say?*

Stay silent and wait patiently. Usually a person staring into the distance is lost in thought. However long it takes to find an answer, give your coachee the gift of space and time to think.

7   *As I start to repeat something back, the coachee starts talking again before I have a chance to ask the question. What should I do?*

Coachees are really thinking out loud. Since the information is for their benefit, add it to your notes, and then you're back on track. Repeat the last thing said and ask the question you were planning to ask.

8   *The coachee's answers are really long. Do I have to use everything they say when I ask the next questions?*

No. Some people think out loud. So their first words are not their final words (e.g. 'Well I need to try to talk to ... If I could sit down with the team ... What I *need* to do is arrange a meeting and present my ideas'). They've just clarified something for themselves. You note down and repeat back the final piece they've said: 'And you need to arrange a meeting and present your ideas', rather than everything they said. Then ask your next question.

If the long answer is at the end of Stage 3, in response to 'Given what you *now* know, what would you like to have happen?' see FAQ 42.

9 ***Sometimes, when I follow the Five-Minute Coach method as described, the questions I should be asking are quite ungrammatical. Can I change the grammar so the questions sound right?***

As a general rule you do not change the grammar. There are exceptions. You can address the coachee as 'you' rather than repeating 'I' and 'me'. In Stages 2 and 5, as you have read, you change verbs from future tense to present, such that 'I want to improve department performance' is repeated back as 'And when you improve department performance ...'

Questions that sound ungrammatical still make perfect sense to the coachee, and it's easier for her to answer the question when it's expressed in the same words she used. Remember your aim is to support the coachee to achieve her outcome, not to get an A in English!

10 ***In response to a question the coachee says, 'I don't know.' What should I do?***

Wait in silence, without making eye contact. For some people, this is an almost automatic response before they answer a question. If the coachee hasn't responded after you've counted to 10, then follow the varying instructions at each stage below.

Managing yourself

11 ***The coachee has answered using metaphor and I don't really know what it means. What do I do?***

You don't need to understand what your coachee is talking about. Metaphor is a rich and useful way to describe complex matters concisely. If you listen carefully you'll hear metaphor in all conversations. Just work with the metaphor and ask questions about it in the same way as you would about a non-metaphorical statement.

12 ***Once I've written down a lot of things the coachee has said, I lose track of what I should be asking about. What can I do?***

Highlight or underline the information that you need to come back to – this includes the outcome that you develop at each of Stages 1–3, as well as the word or phrase in Stage 3 that you choose to ask questions about.

It's also helpful to note the question you've just asked in the left-hand margin of the paper, so you remember what you asked. You could do this in a shortened or acronym form if necessary (e.g. 'And what would you *like* to have happen?' becomes 'WLH?' or 'What kind of ...?' becomes 'WKO?'). You'll see an example of this in the handwritten notes in Appendix II.

13 ***The coachee speaks really quickly. I can't get everything written down. What do I do?***

You can slow your coachee down by repeating the words out loud as you note them. Most people are very polite and will slow down, almost dictating for you. If you feel too bashful to speak out loud as you note the words, write down key phrases and repeat those back before asking your next question.

14 ***The coachee's answers are really long. How do I write them all down?***

You don't have to. You may need to develop a form of shorthand, including abbreviating words. Don't worry that your coachee may not understand your shorthand. You hand over your notes to reassure the coachee that you're not keeping a record of what was said. It adds to the message you gave about the confidentiality of a session. If you have to miss out words, do your best to capture a few key words from each sentence – things that sound significant to you or that you can tell seem to be important based on the coachee's intonation, gestures or general body movements. Typically key words can be about metaphors, action words or feelings.

15 ***The coachee's answers are really long and I found I stopped listening for a short while. How do I prevent this?***

If you make notes as the coachee speaks, even if you can't get *everything* written down, it will help your concentration. If you do lose focus, start listening again as soon as you notice. Then, when you ask your next question, repeat the last words you heard your coachee say.

16 ***I repeat back what was just said but get one or two words wrong, and the coachee looks at me blankly. What do I do?***

Repeat what you think was said – in a questioning tone – and wait some more. The coachee will usually respond to the implied question. If not, repeat again what you think was said and ask your next question.

17 ***When I repeat back what I think was said, the coachee corrects me and looks quite irritated. What do I do next?***

Keep your expression neutral and your voice even. Repeat exactly what the coachee just said and ask your next question. You cannot be sure the look is one of irritation. If it is irritation, you don't know whether the cause is you or something else. Either way, you are not responsible for how the coachee feels.

18 ***The coachee expresses discomfort with this coaching approach. How do I react?***

Your best response is to acknowledge what's just been said and hand the choice back: 'And [you feel uncomfortable with this approach], and what would you like to have happen?' If the coachee wants to do something different, and you are at Stage 1 or 2 of the process, ask whether you can continue for just five more minutes. In our experience, once engaged in the Five-Minute Coach process, a coachee becomes absorbed and really enjoys the benefits of this way of coaching.

Stage 1 Troubleshooting FAQs

Stage 1: Identifying an outcome	**And what would you like to have happen?**

Keeping ownership with the coachee

19 *In response to, 'What would you like to have happen?' the coachee has asked me to suggest an answer. Now what do I say?*

At this point you make a statement, but you do it in a Five-Minute Coach way. So if the coachee says, 'I'd like you to advise what I should do', you respond with: 'And you'd like me to advise. And I can't advise. And when I *can't* advise, what would you like to have happen?'

Managing the process

20 *The coachee says, 'I don't want ...' rather than 'I want ...' What do I do next?*

You repeat the answer and ask your question again. For instance: 'And when you *don't* want to be ignored, what *would* you like to have happen?'

21 *The coachee wants to be less stressed. But it's less of something that's already a problem, such as stress. Do I take this as the outcome?*

In the Five-Minute Coach, you can treat this as an outcome. After all, the coachee has said, 'I want ...' So work with that, and ask, 'And when you are less stressed, then what happens?'

22 ***When I ask the outcome question about a coachee's
    problem, I discover more and more problems but no
    mention of an outcome. What do I do?***

Repeat the latest answer and ask your question again, maybe
emphasising a different word in your question. For example,
'And when [last answer], what would you *like* to have happen?'
If you've asked this question three times, and your coachee
still hasn't described an outcome, you can ask: 'And when [last
answer], what would you like instead?'

23 ***The outcome seems to be out of the coachee's sphere of
    influence. How do I respond?***

Use the 'And can ...?' question (from Stage 4). For example,
respond to 'I want my boss to be more considerate' with
'And can your boss be more considerate?' If the coachee says
'yes', continue to Stage 2. If the answer is 'no' or a weak
'yes', acknowledge what the coachee wants, and that it's not
possible, and ask for another outcome. You do this by asking:
'And you want your boss to be more considerate, and your
boss can't be more considerate. And when your boss can't be
more considerate what would you like to have happen?' When
you have an outcome that is within the coachee's sphere of
influence, move to Stage 2.

24 ***When I ask the question, the coachee just says, 'I don't
    know.' What do I do?***

See FAQ 10. You still need to ascertain an outcome, and you
need to acknowledge that at the moment the coachee doesn't
know. So you ask: 'And when you don't know, what would you
like to have happen?' If you hear 'I'd like to know' then you
have an outcome and can continue to Stage 2 and ask: 'And
when you know, then what happens?'

Managing yourself

25 ***The outcome expressed by the coachee is unrealistic and
unachievable. What do I say?***

You ask the usual Five-Minute Coach questions, using a tone
of voice that indicates the outcome is perfectly realistic and
achievable. Let the coachee reach her own conclusion, either
during the coaching session or afterwards, and if necessary
revise her outcome.

Stage 2 Troubleshooting FAQs

Stage 2: Choosing the best outcome	**And when** [outcome in coachee's words], ***then* what happens?**
	And when [last answer], ***then* what happens?** (Repeat question, with each answer, until no new answers emerge)
	And [outcome] **and** [recap all answers], **what are you drawn to most?**

Keeping ownership with the coachee

26 ***When I ask, 'And what are you drawn to most?' the coachee
can't decide and asks my opinion. What do I do?***

You know your opinion isn't relevant. So if, for example, your
coachee says: 'I'm not sure what draws me most. What do you
think I should go for?', shrug and repeat the last part of your
question slowly: 'And what are *you* drawn to most?' You've
underlined the fact that you're not answering questions
during the coaching session and you've handed the decision-
making back to her.

Managing the process

27 **The coachee has answered the question from this stage three times already. How do I know when to stop asking the question?**

Only stop when the coachee does one of the following three things:

- Starts to repeat answers.

- Gives answers that include words like 'happy', 'fulfilled' or 'satisfied'.

- States clearly 'That's it/all'.

28 **In response to the question my coachee says something that sounds negative, such as, 'Then I feel awful!' Do I continue to ask, 'And then what happens?'**

No. At this point you ask the Stage 1 question: 'And when you feel awful, what would you like to have happen?' When you have an answer stating what the coachee wants, continue to ask, 'And then what happens?'

29 **It was all going really well, and then the coachee started to notice a problem with the consequences that emerged. What do I do?**

Pat yourself on the back. Your coachee has identified a problem during the safety of a coaching session. Now she has the opportunity to think again about her outcome. For example, the coachee says, 'Then my workload reduces ... but I'm concerned that might make it easy to make me redundant.' You say, 'And when your workload reduces but you're concerned that might make it easy to make you redundant, what would you *like* to have happen?' The coachee replies, 'My workload reduces *and* my boss values what I do enough that my job is safe.' And you say, 'And when your workload reduces *and* your boss values what you do enough that your job is safe, *then* what happens?' You now have a consequence the coachee wants and so are back on track in Stage 2.

30 **When I'm recapping, should I mention the bits where the coachee wasn't happy with something and then chose another consequence?**

No. For instance, in the example in FAQ 28 above, you ignore the first statement 'feel awful', and only feed back the key points from the second statement where the coachee told you what she *wanted*.

31 **We were at the very end of this stage and my coachee's response to, 'And what are you drawn to most?' was something she didn't want – a problem. What do I do?**

You know she needs an outcome in order to proceed with the Five-Minute Coach process. So simply ask, 'And when [problem] what would you *like* to have happen?' For example, in response to 'And when [outcome and recap all answers], what are you drawn to most?' the coachee says: 'I don't want to be at risk of redundancy,' you say, 'And when you don't want to be at risk of redundancy, what would you like to have happen?' The coachee's answer, if stated as an outcome, is what you use in Stage 3. If it's another problem, keep asking, 'And when [problem] what would you like to have happen?' until you get an outcome for the next stage.

32 **After asking all these questions the coachee has still chosen the very first outcome. What do I do?**

You trust that the coachee has fully explored the consequences of what she wants and is satisfied with the original outcome. Move on to Stage 3 using that outcome.

Managing yourself

33 **I keep getting more, new answers to the question but I am concerned the coachee may be getting annoyed with me continually asking. When can I stop?**

If you have not heard an answer such as those outlined above (being happy, fulfilled, satisfied or a sense of finality), then ask one more time *after* you have started to feel uncomfortable.

34 *I asked the question several times until the coachee answered, 'Then I die.' How do I respond?*

It's OK. You haven't yet heard one of the three things described in FAQ 27. So continue asking the Stage 2 question in the normal way: 'And when you die, then what happens?'

35 *In response to a question the coachee says, 'I don't know' in a worried tone and looks at me waiting for me to respond. What do I do?*

See FAQ 10. The coachee's discovery that she doesn't yet know something can be very valuable input for her. Allow time for this information to be absorbed and processed. If the silence continues after you've taken two slow breaths, ask, 'And you don't know, and what would you like to have happen?' When you have an answer stating what she wants, continue to ask, 'And then what happens?'

Stage 3 Troubleshooting FAQs

Stage 3: Discovering more about the outcome	**And when** [new outcome], **what kind of** [word or phrase from outcome]?
	And when [last answer], **is there anything else about** [same word or phrase]?
	And when [last answer], **where is/are** [same word or phrase]?
	And when [last answer], **whereabouts** [last answer]?
	And [last answer]. **Given what you *now* know, what would you like to have happen?**

Managing the process

36   *How do I know which word or short phrase to ask the Stage 3 questions about?*

Most, if not all, words will yield further information for the coachee when these questions are asked. If you are uncertain which to choose, it is often useful to ask the questions about a feeling, an action word or a metaphor. Alternatively, select a word that seemed most important to the coachee because it was repeated, or was said with emphasis or more loudly. A tip from experienced Five-Minute Coaches is that short words can be as useful as long words.

37   *In response to my question, the coachee says, 'I don't know.' What do I ask next?*

See FAQ 10. If you still do not hear an answer, repeat what the coachee just said, and move to your next question: 'And you don't know and [your next question]?' Repeating back 'I don't know' in an even voice is like repeating any other answer and helps the coachee continue to reflect more deeply.

38   *The coachee says she can't answer the 'where' question. What do I do?*

See FAQ 10. Your role is to ask the question. If she can't answer move on calmly using whatever words you heard – as though the response is perfectly normal. For example: 'And when you can't answer, whereabouts (return to same word or phrase because you have no answer to "where")?'

39   *The coachee says she can't answer the 'whereabouts' questions. What do I do?*

As in FAQ 38: 'And you can't answer. Given what you now know, what would you like to have happen?'

Managing yourself

40 **Sometimes the 'where' or 'whereabouts' questions just seem irrelevant. Can I ignore them?**

No. You need to ask *all* four questions in the sequence given. The coachee can choose how, or whether, to respond. There are sometimes occasions when a coachee doesn't expect this question to be relevant and then discovers really useful information. The only time you can avoid asking the 'whereabouts' question is when you've asked the "where" question and the coachee says something like 'It doesn't have a location.'

Stage 4 Troubleshooting FAQs

Stage 4: Action planning	**And what needs to happen for** [final outcome]**?**
	And is there anything else that needs to happen for [final outcome]**?** (Repeat question until you hear first 'no')
	And [final outcome and recap every action point]**, and is there anything else that needs to happen for** [final outcome]**?** (Repeat question until you hear second 'no')
	And [final outcome and recap every action point]**, and what needs to happen *first*?**
	And can [previous answer]**?**

Keeping ownership with the coachee

41 *The action plan seems to be full of actions that are outside the coachee's sphere of influence, such as 'the director needs to change his attitude.' What do I do?*

This is usually an issue only if the coachee says that the first thing that needs to happen *can't* happen. If the first thing *can* happen – you hear a strong 'yes' – then continue with the Five-Minute Coach questions. If the answer is 'no' or a weak 'yes', the coachee will need a second or even a third action plan.

If, after all this, you still get a 'no', because the action is actually outside the coachee's sphere of influence, then reflect that back, slowly and deliberately, as follows: 'And [first thing that needs to happen] and it can't, and [*second* 'first thing' that needs to happen] – and it can't – and [*third* 'first thing' that needs to happen] – and it can't – and what would you like to have happen?' Make sure that you slow down each time you say 'and it can't'. With the answer to this question, which is more likely to be within the coachee's control, run through the whole Five-Minute Coach sequence from Stage 1.

Managing the process

42 *The coachee's outcome is very lengthy and it takes me a long time to keep asking it in full every time I ask a question. Can I shorten it?*

Unfortunately not! These particular words mean something to your coachee in exactly the way they've been phrased. Repeat her words, slowly and deliberately, each time you ask your question. Of course, if you notice that the coachee later shortens it, then you can use the shortened version.

43 *At the end of this stage the coachee can't do the first thing that needs to happen. What do I do?*

If you hear a 'no' or a weak 'yes', ask the action planning questions of the first thing that needs to happen (see Figure 9 in Chapter 6). Start at the beginning of Stage 4: 'And what needs to happen for [first thing that needs to happen]?' Then create a whole action plan for this first thing. If necessary, repeat this step – create a further action plan – until the coachee has a first thing that *can* be done. If you run out of time before that happens, offer another coaching session.

44 *In response to, 'And is there anything else that needs to happen?', the coachee says, 'I don't know.' What do I ask next?*

See FAQ 10. Then treat this as your first 'no'. Recap the outcome and all the action points you've heard to date and ask the question again. Usually the coachee will have another action point.

45 *In response to, 'And can …?' the coachee says, 'I don't know.' What do I do?*

See FAQ 10. Then treat this as a 'no' and create an action plan for the first thing that needs to happen, as described in Chapter 6.

Managing yourself

46 *I am concerned that I am irritating the coachee by asking the same question over and over again. What can I do?*

Notice that this is *your* concern. Learn to trust the Five-Minute Coach process. When you've done this a few times you realise that coachees find your persistence useful. It encourages them to seek every possible action that would help them achieve their outcomes. Remember, the decision is always theirs. If they're irritated they can tell you. Until then, stay with the process.

47 ***With my experience I could offer some really useful input to the coachee. How do I do this?***

You don't! The Five-Minute Coach is designed to help the coachee find a personally tailored way to achieve the chosen outcome. If, after a session is finished, the coachee asks for your input, feel free to offer the benefit of your experience. Otherwise, as coach, keep your counsel.

48 ***The coachee's action plan seems to be missing some obvious steps. What do I do?***

Trust that the coachee knows best, unless you believe there is an issue of safety. Continue to go through the Five-Minute Coach process, as described, and notice what happens. You might be pleasantly surprised. If necessary, the coachee can always ask for more coaching if the action plan doesn't seem to be working.

Stage 5 Troubleshooting FAQs

Stage 5: Motivate to act	**And when** [first thing]**, then what happens?** (Repeat until coachee is in a positive state and seems keen to act)
	And is that a good place to stop? (Hand over notes)

Managing the process

49 ***The coachee has answered the question from this stage
three times already. How do I know when to stop asking
the question?***

When your coachee is genuinely positive, motivated and
enthusiastic, then stop! As a rule of thumb, when you think
it's time to stop, ask the question one last time.

Managing yourself

50 ***The coachee already seems motivated to get started. Do I
still need to go to through this stage?***

If this is a full coaching session then yes! Your questions
enable the coachee to experience the outcome as if she's
already achieved it.

Chapter 9

Coaching in Action

As you've read in Chapter 8, not every Five-Minute Coach session goes exactly to plan, although many do. In this chapter we present you with a transcript of a coaching session between a coach and Sunita, where at times Sunita's answers don't lead the coach directly to the next sequential question or stage. Instead, the coach has to choose which questions to ask to get the coaching back on a positive path through the Five-Minute Coach framework.

You can read here the questions asked, Sunita's responses and, most importantly, the thoughts, choices and decisions made by the coach after each response. If until now you had feared that the coach did not have a leading role in this coaching, you'll see exactly how important it is for the coach to steer things through the process to keep the coaching on a positive – and useful – path, with well-placed questions.

Coach: Hello Sunita! And where would you like to sit (gesturing around the space)?

(Sunita sits down)

And where would you like me to sit?

Sunita: There's fine (points and coach sits down).

Coach: Let me explain a little about this coaching. My role here is to help you explore your issue, work out what you want and how you are going to achieve it. I won't be offering you ideas or suggestions as to how to do it.

You'll soon find that this isn't like a normal conversation or even any coaching session you may have had before. I won't look at you much and I won't make any suggestions or comments about what you say.

I will be taking notes to help me remember what you say. And, at the end, I'll give you all the notes.

Anything you say is confidential, unless it's illegal or unsafe.

If I ask you any questions that seem unusual or odd, just answer with the first thing that comes to mind.

Once we start, I won't be answering any questions as that will interrupt the flow. So ... is there anything you'd like to ask me now?

Sunita: No.

Coach	Sunita	
And what would you like to have happen?	The reorganisation to finish now, and my job to be safe.	
And *can* the reorganisation finish now and your job be safe**?**	Well, the reorganisation can't finish right now – and I've no idea about my job!	
And when you want the reorganisation to finish and your job to be safe **(slow down next words)** *and* it can't, *and* you've no idea about your job**, (pause) what would you like to have happen?**	I don't want to lose my job.	
And when you don't want to lose your job, **what would you *like* to have happen?**	Well, it's important that I earn enough money.	
And when you earn enough money, *then* **what happens?**	Then I can pay the bills and be free from worry. You've no idea how hard it's been ... waiting to hear whether I've got a job or not.	

Behind the scenes (inside the coach's head)
This Stage 1 outcome seems to be outside Sunita's control. I suppose I'd better check with the 'can' question – in case she thinks it is within her control.
Well, I was right, it's definitely outside her control! Let me reflect back, nice and slowly, so she gets the point that it's outside her control. Then I can ask for another outcome that is within her control.
She's said what she doesn't want. So let's see if I can find out what she does want by asking the outcome question again.
Is this an outcome? I think I can use it as an outcome for us to work on – she wants to earn enough money. Now we're ready for Stage 2.
OK, now I've got consequences (paying the bills and being free from worry) and a comment about how hard it's been. I can ignore the comment and just keep testing whether she's going to be happy with the consequences.

Coach	Sunita	
And when you pay the bills **(slow down next words) and** you're free from worry, ***then* what happens?**	Do you mean immediately afterwards …. Or longer term? (looking expectantly)	
Yes.	Well, immediately … and longer term, I suppose … when I can pay the bills … I have time, a cushion, to discover what I really want to do with my life.	
And when you have time, a cushion **(slow down next words) and** you discover what you really want to do with your life, ***then* what happens?**	That would be wonderful because then I finally have the chance to live the life I want. In fact, it would be fantastic.	
And when you live the life you want …	Yes, it would be more than fantastic. It would be tremendous to have money to do things like the travelling I've always dreamt of. And I'd be able to take up some of the hobbies that I've had to give up over the years, because they were too expensive. Yes, I really would be free from worry.	
And when it's tremendous, and money to do things like travelling and you … (tailing off expectantly, whilst writing notes).	… have time to take up some of my old hobbies … because I'd be free of worries.	

Behind the scenes (inside the coach's head)
Oh dear! She's asked me a question ... and I'm not supposed to engage with her. I wonder if I was engaging her in eye contact. Anyway, let me look away now ... keep silent ... count to 10 ... and hope she comes up with something. *Still nothing from her. Keep calm! I'll give her an ambivalent answer.*
Phew! That worked. That's a consequence that she seems happy with. Let's keep going.
Whoa! That's a big change in her tempo and mood. I wonder what just happened for her. Maybe it was the way I slowed down, so she absorbed the benefits of a cushion of time. Anyway, thank goodness I don't need to know the ins and outs. Now I will keep asking this same question to unroll the full consequences of this outcome.
Definitely hit her enthusiasm there! She didn't even let me finish my question. Still, I'll use what she's given me and ask what I was going to ask. *Oh no, so busy talking to myself, I didn't write down all she said. Fingers crossed ... if I repeat what I've got and pause, she'll fill in the gaps.*
Thank you, Sunita! Onto the next consequence!

Coach	Sunita
And when it's tremendous, and money to do travelling, and you take up some of your old hobbies, and you're free from worry, ***then* what happens?**	Then I have time for family and friends as well as things for myself. The only thing is … then I might become too selfish … focusing only on myself. Hmm … that's not so good.
And you have time for your family and friends as well as things for yourself, *and* you might become too selfish, **(slow down next words) and what would you like to have happen?**	I'd like to have time for family, friends, me *and* do some good in the world too.
And when you have time for family, and friends, and you *and* do some good in the world, ***then* what happens?**	Then I'm happy!
And when you're happy, ***then* what happens?**	Nothing else. I'm just happy.

Behind the scenes (inside the coach's head)

Oh dear! What do I do now? Let me stay calm and remember what I need to do!

It's fine! She's identified a potential problem. Let's get it sorted by feeding it back in my next question. Then she can work out what to do and make an informed choice.

Excellent, she has made her choice and is moving forward. Let's keep exploring the consequences.

That sounds good. But it's not up to me. So I'll ask the question again to find out if there are any further consequences.

As I suspected, she has gone as far as she can with this question and is satisfied with the consequences. Now I need to find out if any of the consequences might become a new outcome for her.

Coach	Sunita
And when you earn enough money and you can pay the bills and you're free from worry; you have time, a cushion, you discover what you really want to do with your life; you live the life you want and it's tremendous, you're free from worry; you have time for family and friends and yourself *and* do some good in the world, (slow down next words) and you're happy, **what are you drawn to most?**	Earning enough money.
And when earning 'enough' money, **what kind of** 'enough'**?**	I don't know.
	... Enough to cover all the bills and have some over, so I needn't worry.
And enough to cover all the bills and have some over. **And when** enough, **is there anything else about** enough**?**	Yes ... enough is satisfying.
And when enough is satisfying, **where is** enough**?**	What do you mean – where is enough?

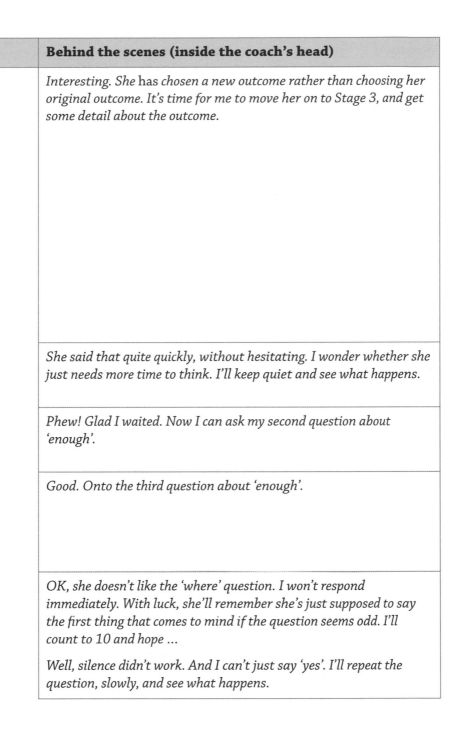

Behind the scenes (inside the coach's head)
Interesting. She has chosen a new outcome rather than choosing her original outcome. It's time for me to move her on to Stage 3, and get some detail about the outcome.
She said that quite quickly, without hesitating. I wonder whether she just needs more time to think. I'll keep quiet and see what happens.
Phew! Glad I waited. Now I can ask my second question about 'enough'.
Good. Onto the third question about 'enough'.
OK, she doesn't like the 'where' question. I won't respond immediately. With luck, she'll remember she's just supposed to say the first thing that comes to mind if the question seems odd. I'll count to 10 and hope … *Well, silence didn't work. And I can't just say 'yes'. I'll repeat the question, slowly, and see what happens.*

Coach	Sunita	
And when enough is satisfying, **(slow down next words)** *where* **is** enough?	Oh … you said you weren't going to answer my questions, didn't you. OK … the first thing that comes to my head … enough is in my gut.	
And when enough is in your gut, **whereabouts** in your gut?	It's silly! OK … enough is right in the middle of my gut.	
And enough is right in the middle of your gut. **Given what you** *now* **know, what would you like to have happen?**	I want to earn enough and have satisfaction.	
And what needs to happen for you to earn enough and have satisfaction?	I don't know … hmm, that's difficult …	
	… I suppose, whilst they're thinking about reorganising and I'm waiting to find out if I have a job … I could write out to my contacts and sound out what kind of jobs and consultancy are out there.	
And is there anything else that needs to happen for you to earn enough and have satisfaction?	I could work out my expenses, see whether there's anything we could pare down, so I know what enough is.	
And is there anything else that needs to happen for you to earn enough and have satisfaction?	I could make a list of all the things that I enjoy doing … see if there's anything that could turn into paid work.	

Behind the scenes (inside the coach's head)
Good! I don't fully understand the answer, but that doesn't matter. At some level it means something to Sunita. Thank goodness it doesn't have to make sense to me. I'll just move onto the 'whereabouts' question and see what she makes of that.
She's going with the flow. Great! Now my summary question for this stage.
Great – we have a final outcome. Now, let's move to Stage 4 and get Sunita an action plan.
She's said 'I don't know' before and then did come up with an answer. So let me try silence again.
Well, that worked! I'll ask the action planning question again.
OK. I still haven't heard my first 'no', so I'd better keep asking this question.
Good thinking! And I need to ask the same question again.

Coach	Sunita	
And is there anything else that needs to happen for you to earn enough and have satisfaction**?**	I don't think so.	
And to earn enough and have satisfaction, write out to your contacts and sound out what kind of jobs and consultancy is out there; and work out your expenses to see what you could pare down and what is enough; and make a list of all the things you enjoy doing to see if anything could turn into paid work. **And is there anything else that needs to happen for you to earn enough and have satisfaction?**	I suppose I could talk to my partner … share our ideas for how to go forward.	
And is there anything else that needs to happen for you to earn enough and have satisfaction**?**	No.	

Behind the scenes (inside the coach's head)
OK, I've waited. I've counted to 10. She's not going to say any more. So there's my first 'no'. Now I need to summarise and ask again.
Yes, that's a good idea. She hasn't said her second 'no' yet so I must ask the question yet again. I wonder how many more actions there could be. I must make sure I write them all down as I'll never remember.
Well, that was quick. She suddenly got to the second 'no'. I must summarise again and then ask about the first thing to start off the whole action plan.

Coach	Sunita
And to earn enough and have satisfaction, write out to your contacts, sound out what kind of jobs and consultancy are out there; work out your expenses, see what you could pare down and what is enough; and make a list of all the things you enjoy doing to see if anything could turn into paid work; and talk to your partner and share your ideas for how to go forward. **And what needs to happen first?**	I need to sit down with my partner and work out what we need to do to jointly earn enough to be happy.
And can you sit down with your partner and work out what you need to do to jointly earn enough to be happy**?**	Hmm ... I think so.
And what needs to happen for you to sit down with your partner and work out what you need to do to jointly to earn enough to be happy**?**	I need to arrange some quiet, quality time, with no distractions, to talk things through. That's difficult with the kids around.
And is there anything else that needs to happen for you to sit down with your partner and work out what you need to do jointly to earn enough to be happy**?**	I need to check what we both think that 'happy' is.

Behind the scenes (inside the coach's head)
There it is – a starting point! Good! Let me check she can do it.
Whoa! That's not really a yes. And she sounded quite hesitant. So I must assume this is a 'no'. Stay calm. What to do next? *Well, if she can't do this first step, then she needs an action plan so that she can do it. If we don't get an actionable starting point then she's not going to get her outcome. So let's go through the Stage 4 action planning questions for this first thing she needs to do.*
OK, got an action point. She's said it's difficult ... but I'm going to let that go, and stick to the process.
Let me ask the question again until I get my first 'no' for this action plan.

Coach	Sunita	
And is there anything else that needs to happen for you to sit down with your partner and work out what you need to do jointly to earn enough to be happy**?**	No.	
And to sit down with your partner and work out what you need to do jointly to earn enough to be happy, you need to arrange some quiet, quality time to talk things through, and you need to check what you both think that happy is. **And is there anything else that needs to happen for** you to sit down with your partner and work out what you need to do jointly to earn enough to be happy**?**	No.	
And to sit down with your partner and work out what you need to do jointly to earn enough to be happy, you need to arrange some quiet, quality time to talk things through, and you need to check what you both think that happy is; and you need to be honest with each other about whether your work makes you happy. **And what needs to happen first?**	We need to set up an honesty session.	

Behind the scenes (inside the coach's head)
Got it! Now I need to recap and ask again until I get my second 'no'.
OK, second 'no'. So let me move on to finding the first step of this action plan.
OK. Now we've got the first step for this sub-action plan – let's just check that she can do it. Fingers crossed!

Coach	Sunita	
And can you set up an honesty session**?**	Yes!	
And when you set up an honesty session, ***then* what happens?**	Then we create a strong base for the future, no matter how difficult it could become. What I don't want is for one of us to become a martyr ... because we haven't been honest that we don't like what we're doing. After all, money could be tight and that's sometimes what scuppers relationships.	
And when you have a firm foundation for the future ...	A strong base!	
And when you have a strong base for the future, **then what happens?**	Then we can build anything on that base, and so we can be flexible about what we do, how much we earn, whether we work part time or full time.	
And when you can build anything on that base, **then what happens?**	Then we can be financially and emotionally independent. No one can hold us to ransom!	
And when you're financially and emotionally independent, (slow down next words) and no one can hold you to ransom, **then what happens?**	Then we're a fabulous example to the kids too. And other people envy us, and want to do the same thing!	
And is that a good place to stop?	Yes!	

Behind the scenes (inside the coach's head)
Fantastic! Finished the action plan. Now I need to move to Stage 5 to help her do a mental rehearsal and get enthused about doing this first step.
Whoa! Lots of information there. I'll recap a key point and ask then what happens.
OK, OK, I got the words wrong! I almost apologised but I remember I am not supposed to. So I'll use the corrected words and keep going.
She's definitely sounding more enthusiastic. I wonder if I ask her the question again will I get any more from her. I'll try.
That sounds positive. I wonder if she's finished. I'll ask again to find out.
She's beaming now. Seems like a good time to stop and let her get started with her first action point from her 'strong base'!
Now all that's left is to hand over her notes. Well done, me!

Chapter 10
Building Your Skills

There are many ways in which to build your skills in using the Five-Minute Coach. Here are a few practical ideas – some things to try out with others and some exercises that you can work through on your own.

Buddy practice

Many trainee Five-Minute Coaches find it useful to find someone to practise with. Co-coaching a buddy who is also learning to coach this way is a safe and fast way for you both to develop your skills. If you have more than one buddy then work in a group of three, with one as coach, one as coachee and one as observer giving feedback at the end of the session. This will accelerate learning, increase confidence and build enthusiasm.

We recommend that you schedule regular get-togethers, allowing enough time for each of you to take a turn at coaching and being coached. Experiencing the Five-Minute Coach, as a coachee, is very valuable. Not only do you get the benefits of a great coaching session, but you also have a much richer understanding of being on the receiving end of this style of coaching. People find that the experience dispels many of their worries and concerns about the impact of some of the more unusual aspects, such as ungrammatical questions, lack of discussion, limited eye contact and repetitive questioning.

Although you'd ideally meet face to face when you first learn the Five-Minute Coach, this coaching will work via telephone or video conferencing too. If you need a hand to find a practice buddy, email coach@thefiveminutecoach.co.uk asking to be connected to other trainee Five-Minute Coaches.

Exercises

In addition to the two practice activities in each of Chapters 3–7 of this book, here are a range of exercises to improve your command of the Five-Minute Coach. The answers, which you'll find at the end of the chapter, are the simplest possible, based on what you've read in this book. If you've had any Clean Language training, then you know that other answers could be valid.

The twelve exercises have been designed to help you learn different things. We have categorised them in the following way:

Exercises 1–5	Basic responses at different stages
Exercises 6–8	Somewhat trickier situations
Exercises 9–10	Issues where you may need to pose questions out of sequence
Exercises 11–12	Practising the nuance of emphasis

Exercise 1

Related to: Stage 1 – identifying an outcome

Exercise type: work by yourself

Purpose: to practise asking your next question when the response doesn't tell you very clearly what the coachee wants, and to note when silence might be your co-coach

Imagine that you ask a coachee:

And what would you like to have happen?

You receive the following responses. In each case, what exactly do you do or ask next?

1   I don't know if I can answer 'What would you like to have happen?'

2   Either cope with the stress of this job, or settle for earning less in another job.

3   I'm not sure whether I want this job.

4   I don't know what to do about this problem.

5   There's so much I want, I don't know where to start.

6   My boss says I should change my approach ... or move jobs.

7   It's a big mess. I really don't know what to do ... What do you think I should do?

8   I really can't be sure that what I want is the right thing.

9   I wish I knew.

10 I have a dilemma ... do I stay or leave?

Exercise 2

Related to: Stage 1 – identifying an outcome

Exercise type: work by yourself

Purpose: to practise dealing with a response that only describes what a coachee doesn't want

Hint: You need to have something the coachee does want before you can move to Stage 2

Imagine that you ask a coachee:

And what would you like to have happen?

You get the following responses. What do you ask next?

1   I don't want to work such long hours.

2   I'd rather not have to deal with such difficult situations without proper support.

3   I don't care what happens to me, but I don't want my staff to suffer.

4   I don't know what to do about the backlog.

5   My business can't be vulnerable.

6   I can't stand working for my boss.

7   I don't want to feel so stressed.

8   It's important that I don't make a mistake about a crucial decision I need to make.

9   Staff in my department are really unhelpful.

10 I don't get proper recognition of my contribution.

Exercise 3

Related to: Stage 2 – choosing the best outcome

Exercise type: work by yourself

Purpose: to practise asking your next question once the coachee gives you an outcome

Whether part of formal coaching sessions or informal exchanges, imagine that you hear each of the following statements. In every case you wish to ask the other person the next Five-Minute Coach question. What exactly do you ask next?

1   I need to learn a new skill.

2   I want a promotion.

3   More recognition.

4   I have to find another job.

5   Set up on my own.

6   My priority has got to be earning more.

7   I wish I could find a way to make more time for myself.

8   I'm supposed to molly-coddle my team.

9   I would like to feel less frustrated by my boss.

10 I would love to manage a team.

Exercise 4

Related to: Stage 3 – discovering more

Exercise type: work by yourself

Purpose: to practise asking the 'whereabouts' question

You receive the following answers to 'And where is ...?' In each case, what do you ask next?

1 **Where is** 'respect'**?**

   It's on the table.

2 **Where is** 'want'**?**

   Want is in my hands.

3 **Where is** 'tree'**?**

   It's outside, in the garden.

4 **Where is** 'whole'**?**

   It could be anywhere.

5 **Where is** 'project'**?**

   Working together.

6 **Where is** 'prioritise'**?**

   Prioritise is at my desk.

7 **Where is** 'knowing'**?**

   In any challenging moment.

8 **Where is** 'enjoy'**?**

   It's after the goal.

9 **Where is** 'everything'**?**

   Social situations ... by myself.

10 **Where is** 'I'**?**

   I is on a hill top.

Exercise 5

Related to: Stage 4 – action planning

Exercise type: work by yourself

Purpose: to experience the benefits of asking the 'anything else' question repeatedly, whilst practising your skills

Think of a personal outcome where creating an action plan could be particularly useful to you. Complete the following questions:

> **And what needs to happen for** [your outcome]**?**
>
> **And is there anything *else* that needs to happen for** [your outcome]**?**
>
> **And is there anything *else* that needs to happen for** [your outcome]**?**
>
> **And is there anything *else* that needs to happen for** [your outcome]**?**

Keep answering this question until you believe you have no more answers, writing each answer down in turn. Then, answer:

> **And** [your outcome and recap every action point]**, and is there anything else that needs to happen for** [your outcome]**?**
>
> **And is there *anything* else that needs to happen for** [your outcome]**?**

Keep answering this question until you believe you have no more answers, writing each answer down in turn. Then, answer:

> **And** [your outcome and recap every action point from the start]**, and what needs to happen first?**
>
> **And can** [previous answer]**?**

If 'yes', you now have an action plan. If not, answer:

> **And what needs to happen for** [first thing that needs to happen]**?**

Then develop a whole new action plan using the questions outlined in Figure 9 (Chapter 6).

Exercise 6

Related to: all Five-Minute Coach stages

Exercise type: work by yourself

Purpose: to practise handling 'tricky' situations during coaching

Imagine that in response to a Five-Minute Coach question, you receive the following responses from a coachee. In each case, what would you ask – or do – next?

1   The coachee is silent.

2   I don't know.

   a   When this answer is in response to **'And what would you like to have happen?'**

   b   When this answer is in response to a Stage 3 question, e.g. **'And what kind of** goal**?'**

3   Do you think I should accept the promotion or look for another job?

4   What do you think?

5   Is that OK?

6   It could be wonderful, or it could be awful!

   a   When this answer is in response to **'And then what happens?'**

   b   When this answer is in response to a Stage 3 question, e.g. **'And is there anything else about** goal?'

7   What do you mean ... where is 'being'? (where this was the word or phrase you chose from the outcome at Stage 3.)

8   In response to a 'whereabouts' question, the coachee says: I keep thinking about functionality.

9   In response to **'And what are you drawn to most?'**: It's between prioritising what I have to do, and telling them it's just too big a job.

10   I'm stuck.

Exercise 7

Related to: Stage 1 – identifying an outcome

Exercise type: work by yourself

Purpose: to practise using 'And can ...?' when you think an outcome might be outside the coachee's sphere of influence

In response to the statements below, first phrase your question using 'And can ...?'

What would you then ask if the coachees gave you:

    a   A decisive 'yes'.

    b   A decisive or implied 'no' (an implied 'no' is indicated by a 'yes' said uncertainly or a 'maybe', 'possibly', 'probably', etc.).

1   I want senior managers to change the system.

2   I would like Jon to be more patient with the apprentices.

3   He should take more care of the equipment.

4   The board ought to care more about what staff think.

5   I want the market to get better.

Exercise 8

Related to: end of Stage 4 – first thing that needs to happen
for action plan

Exercise type: work by yourself

Purpose: to practise using 'And can ...?' when you think a
first step might be outside the coachee's sphere of
influence

You've just asked, 'And [latest outcome] and [recap every action
point], and what needs to happen first?', and got the responses
listed below.

First phrase your question using 'And can ...?'

   a   Then what would you ask if the coachee:

   b   Said 'yes'.

Gave you a direct or implied 'no'.

1   Everyone should stick to the timetable.

2   They should give us more information.

3   He needs to take more responsibility for the project.

4   The directors need to be better leaders.

5   Clients should be less demanding.

Exercise 9

Related to: different stages of the Five-Minute Coach

Exercise type: work by yourself

Purpose: to check your grasp of what happens next

Here are a variety of coachee responses that happen at different points of the coaching session. What's your next question or response?

1 **And** you get more time to yourself. **And then what happens?**

   A. Well ... I'd like that .... but I don't want to seem selfish.

2 **And what would you like to have happen?**

   A. I'd love to feel more organised.

3 **And** [latest outcome and recap every action point], **and what needs to happen first?**

   A. My boss should give me more respect for the work I do.

4 **And what would you like to have happen?**

   A. I don't want to keep doing such long hours.

5 **And what would you like to have happen?**

   A. I really want to get this job ... but I'm concerned about the consequences.

6 **And where is** 'difficult'?

   A. For me, it's between a rock and a hard place.

7 **And** [latest outcome and recap every action point], **and what needs to happen first?**

   A. I need to value myself more.

8 **And what would you like to have happen?**

   A. I want an action plan to get the job done.

9   In response to the 'where' question:

A.   It's in my head and my hands.

10   **And what would you like to have happen?**

A.   Hmm ... I'm wondering what I should do about the meeting.

Exercise 10

Related to: all stages of the Five-Minute Coach

Exercise type: work by yourself

Purpose: to practise using these questions whilst in conversation

You hear the following statements in everyday conversation. How would you respond using Five-Minute Coach questions and principles?

1   Do you think I should join a language class or an acting class?

2   I'm supposed to be making this cake, but I don't know where to start.

3   I'm going to change my course. It's the only thing I can do.

4   You need to be more flexible in your approach.

5   I'm worried. He's behaving in a very odd way.

6   I feel life is passing me by!

7   We need to fight this!

8   This place is not organised enough.

9   Look in the cupboard.

10   Your printer can't be repaired. I can replace it with a new printer that is more economical and prints faster.

Exercise 11

Related to: Stage 1 – identifying an outcome

Exercise type: try out with another person

Purpose: to explore how to direct someone's attention more precisely, by varying your emphasis

Ask the coachee to select an issue and then ask the question below, varying only your emphasis. Does the coachee have a different answer when your emphasis changes?

a   **And *what* would you like to have happen?**

b   **And what *would* you like to have happen?**

c   **And what would *you* like to have happen?**

d   **And what would you *like* to have happen?**

e   **And what would you like to *have* happen?**

f   **And what would you like to have *happen*?**

Given the feedback you get, experiment with when to use each 'different' question.

Exercise 12

Related to: Stage 4 – action planning

Exercise type: try out with another person

Purpose: to explore how you can direct someone's attention, with precision, by varying your emphasis

Ask the coachee to select an issue and then ask the question below, varying only your emphasis. Does the coachee have a different answer when your emphasis changes?

a   **And what needs to happen for** [outcome]**?** (no special emphasis) b   **And *is* there anything else that needs to happen for** [outcome]**?**

c   **And is there *anything* else that needs to happen for** [outcome]**?**

d   **And is there anything *else* that needs to happen for** [outcome]**?**

e   **And is there anything else that *needs* to happen for** [outcome]**?**

Given the feedback you get, experiment with when to use each 'different' question.

Answers to exercises

Answers – Exercise 1

In each of these situations, your first response is to keep silent! What follows are your questions if there is still no response after you have begun to feel uncomfortable:

1   **And when** you don't know if you can answer, 'What would you like to have happen?', **what would you *like* to have happen?**

2   **And when** either cope with the stress of this job, or settle for earning less in another job, **what would you *like* to have happen?**

3   **And when** you're not sure whether you want this job, **what would *you* like to have happen?**

4   **And when** you don't know what to do about this problem, **what would you like to have happen?**

5   **And when** there's so much you want, you don't know where to start, **what would you like to have happen?**

6   **And when** your boss says you should change your approach … or move jobs, **what would *you* like to have happen?**

7   **And when** it's a big mess, you don't know what to do, **what would you *like* to have happen?**

8   **And when** you really can't be sure that what you want is the right thing, **what would you like to have happen?**

9   **And** when you wish you knew, **what would you like to have happen?**

10   **And when** you have a dilemma, do you stay or leave, **what would you like to have happen?**

Answers – Exercise 2

1   **And when** you don't want to work such long hours, **what would you *like* to have happen?**

2   **And when** you'd rather not have to deal with such difficult situations without proper support, **what *would* you like to have happen?**

3   **And when** you don't care what happens to you, *but* you don't want your staff to suffer, **what *would* you like to have happen?**

4   **And when** you don't know what to do about the backlog, **what would you *like* to have happen?**

5   **And when** your business can't be vulnerable, **what would you like to have happen?**

6   **And when** you can't stand working for your boss, **what would you like to have happen?**

7   **And when** you don't want to feel so stressed, **what would you like to have happen?**

8   **And when** it's important that you don't make a mistake about a crucial decision you need to make, **what would you like to have happen?**

9 **And when** staff in your department are really unhelpful, **what would you like to have happen?**

10 **And when** you don't get proper recognition of your contribution, **what would you like to have happen?**

Answers – Exercise 3

1 **And when** you learn a new skill, **then what happens?**

2 **And when** you have a promotion, **then what happens?**

3 **And when** more recognition, **then what happens?**

4 **And when** you find another job, **then what happens?**

5 **And when** you set up on your own, **then what happens?**

6 **And when** your priority is earning more, **then what happens?**

7 **And when** you find a way to make more time for yourself, **then what happens?**

8 **And when** you're supposed to molly-coddle your team, **what would *you* like to have happen?** (assuming this is something the person *doesn't* want)

9 **And when** you feel less frustrated by your boss, **then what happens?**

10 **And when** you manage a team, **then what happens?**

Answers – Exercise 4

1 **And when** it's on the table, whereabouts **on the table?**

2 **And when** it's in your hands, whereabouts **in your hands?**

3 **And when** it's outside, in the garden, whereabouts **outside, in the garden?**

4 **And when** it could be anywhere, whereabouts **anywhere?**

5 **And when** working together, whereabouts **working together?**

6 **And when** prioritise is at your desk, whereabouts **at your desk?**

7 **And when** in any challenging moment, whereabouts **in any challenging moment?**

8 **And when** it's after the goal, whereabouts **after the goal?**

9 **And when** social situations ... by yourself, whereabouts **social situations ... by yourself?**

10 **And when** I is on a hill top, whereabouts **on a hill top?**

Answers – Exercise 6

1 Avoid eye contact, if possible. Keep silent and give the coachee space to think. He will ask for further help from you, if he needs it.

2 Stay silent for a little longer than you feel comfortable. If the coachee has still said nothing , ask the question as follows:

   a **And when** you don't know, **what would you *like* to have happen?**

   b **And when** you don't know, **is there anything else about** goal? (You have recapped, and moved on to your next question.)

3 Say 'yes', then avoid eye contact and stay silent. If there is no further response from the coachee, ask as follows: **And when** accept the promotion **or** look for another job, **what would you *like* to have happen?**

4 Avoid eye contact and keep silent for a little longer than you feel comfortable. If the coachee still has not responded, then recap what he said before he asked for your opinion, and ask your next question.

5 Ignore the question. Repeat what the coachee said before she asked if that was OK, and continue as usual.

6   Stay silent for a little longer than you feel comfortable. If the coachee has added nothing further, ask the question as follows:

   a   **And when** it could be wonderful, or it could be awful, **then what happens?**

   b   **And when** it could be wonderful, or it could be awful, **where is** [word or phrase from outcome]**?**

7   Avoid eye contact and stay silent. If there is no further response from the coachee you repeat your question, changing speed and emphasis as follows: **And when** [last answer to **'And is there anything else about** being?'**]**, (slow right down) *where* **is** being**?**

8   **And** you keep thinking about functionality. **And given all you now know, what are you drawn to most?** (You're finishing Stage 3 as normal.)

9   Wait and then ask: **And when** it's between prioritising what you have to do, and telling them it's just too big a job, **what are you drawn to most?**

10   Avoid eye contact and stay silent, a little beyond your discomfort. If necessary ask: **And when** you're stuck, **what would you like to have happen?**

Answers – Exercise 7

1   **And can** senior managers change the system**?**

   a   **And when** senior managers change the system, **then what happens?**

   b   **And** you want senior managers to change the system. **And** senior managers *can't* change the system. **And** when senior managers *can't* change the system, **what would you like to have happen?**

2   **And** can Jon be more patient with the apprentices**?**

   a   **And** when Jon is more patient with apprentices, **then what happens?**

b   **And** you want Jon to be more patient with the apprentices, **and** Jon *can't* be more patient with the apprentices. **And** when Jon *can't* be more patient with the apprentices, **what would you like to have happen?**

3   **And** can he take more care of the equipment**?**

a   **And** when he takes more care of the equipment, **then what happens?**

b   **And** he should take more care of the equipment. **And** he *can't* take more care of the equipment. **And** when he *can't* take more care of the equipment, **what would you like to have happen?**

4   **And** can the board care more about what staff think**?**

a   **And** when the board care more about what staff think, **then what happens?**

b   **And** they can but they won't. **And** when they can, but they won't, **what would you like to have happen?**

5   **And** can the market get better?

a   **And** when the market gets better, **then what happens?**

b   **And** you want the market to get better, **and** you don't know. **And** when you want the market to get better, **and** you don't know, **what would you like to have happen?**

Answers – Exercise 8

1   **And can** everyone stick to the timetable**?**

a   **And** when everyone sticks to the timetable, **then what happens?**

b   **And what needs to happen for** everyone to stick to the timetable**?**

2   **And can** they give you more information**?**

a   **And when** they give you more information, **then what happens?**

b   **And what needs to happen for** them to give you more information**?**

3   **And can** he take more responsibility for the project?

   a   **And when** he takes more responsibility for the project, **then what happens?**

   b   **And what needs to happen for** him to take more responsibility for the project**?**

4   **And can** the directors be better leaders**?**

   a   **And when** the directors are better leaders, **then what happens?**

   b   **And what needs to happen for** the directors to be better leaders**?**

5   **And can** clients be less demanding**?**

   a   **And when** the clients are less demanding, **then what happens?**

   b   **And what needs to happen for** clients to be less demanding**?**

Answers – Exercise 9

1   **And when** you'd like that but you don't want to seem selfish, **what would you like to have happen?** (If the coachee tells you, again, what he doesn't want, recap his latest answer and ask again, **'What would you *like* to have happen?'** If the coachee tells you what he wants, continue to ask, **'And then what happens?'**)

2   **And when** you feel more organised, **then what happens?**

3   **And *can*** your boss give you more respect for the work you do**?** (If the coachee says, 'Yes', continue to Stage 5. If the coachee says, 'She can, but she won't!', you say **'And what needs to happen** for your boss to give you more respect for the work you do?' You are going through the Stage 4 process to get an action plan for this first thing.)

4   **And when** you don't want to keep doing such long hours, **what would you *like* to have happen?**

5 **And when** you really want to get this job, but you're concerned about the consequences, **what would you like to have happen?**

6 **And when** it's between a rock and a hard place, **whereabouts** between a rock and a hard place**?**

7 **And can** you value yourself more**?**

8 **And when** you have an action plan, to get the job done, **then what happens?**

9 **And when** it's in your head and in your hands, **whereabouts** in your head and your hands**?**

10 Keep silent, avoid eye contact, and count to 10. If you still have no response, ask: '**And when you're wondering what you should do about the meeting, what would you like to have happen?**'

Answers – Exercise 10

1 **What are you drawn to most?**

2 **What needs to happen?** or **What needs to happen** for you to make this cake**?** or **What needs to happen** for you to start making this cake**?**

3 **And when** you change your course, **then what happens?**

4 **What kind of** flexible? or When I'm more flexible, **then what happens?**

5 **What kind of** odd? or Hmm ... **and what would you like to have happen?**

6 **What would you like to have happen?**

7 **And, then what happens?** or **What kind of** 'we'**?** or **What kind of** 'fight'**?**

8 **And what would you like to have happen?**

9 **Where** in the cupboard**?**

10 **And is there anything else about** a new printer**?**

Chapter 11

Getting Results with the Five-Minute Coach

Since we first simplified Clean Language and Symbolic Modelling to introduce the Five-Minute Coach to managers, word of its appeal has spread. Now, its methodology and principles are being used in multiple ways within organisations – and in all other areas of life. We are continually discovering innovative and unusual ways in which people are having great success with the Five-Minute Coach, as parents, teachers, volunteers, mediators, designers and more. Here are some examples.

Coaching as a day job

Many professional coaches find the Five-Minute Coach extremely useful in their coaching practice. They appreciate its non-directive, coachee-led approach and find it a very practical and fast way to facilitate people to explore complex issues and create transformation.

Eloise, a self-employed life coach, reports: 'When I first used the Five-Minute Coach it was with a client I had been working with for a while. We had been working on a big dilemma she was facing, and after two sessions we didn't seem to be making great progress. So I used the Five-Minute Coach process and was amazed by the power of these questions – as was the coachee. In no time at all she understood much more about her thinking around the situation, which she hadn't been aware of before. We developed an action plan and next time I saw her she'd made her decision, had started to take action and looked happier than I'd seen her. Now I use the Five-Minute Coach regularly. It keeps me out of the coachee's way and gets incredible results.'

Coaching in-house

Many organisations now train selected employees to be their in-house coaches, to bring the benefits of coaching quickly and cost-effectively into the workplace. Those that are using the Five-Minute Coach as at least one of their coaching approaches are finding it valuable, as it is straightforward to learn and fast to use.

Sayeed, head of coaching at a service company, says: 'One of the problems our internal coaches faced was handling the dual relationship. As part of the business they quite often know not only the person they are coaching, but also the other people mentioned during the coaching and the issues the coachee brings. The Five-Minute Coach has been a great help as it keeps the coach's knowledge, experience and opinions out of the mix. The coaches have told me it is really liberating to have a tool that removes those complications and gives them permission *not* to offer advice or opinions.'

Embedding training

Trainers like to find ways to help people continue to learn and practise skills long after a training programme has finished. Some are now teaching trainees the Five-Minute Coach – so participants can coach each other between modules and after training programmes.

Jennie, a trainer, says: 'We use this now in a range of our learning and development programmes, encouraging our people to coach each other following a training module. That way they apply what they have learned to real business issues. It's been very effective in increasing the impact of the learning.'

Creating productive meetings

The Five-Minute Coach is used in a number of ways in meetings, from setting a shared outcome for the meeting to creating an action plan that all are signed up to.

Kate, a consultant, comments: 'I like to use the Five-Minute Coach when running meetings with my clients. In particular I find the "What kind of ...?" question invaluable in making sure that everyone has the same understanding of things that are being discussed or committed to. One of my clients told me he thought we were on the same wavelength as we never seem to have any misunderstandings. Funny that!'

Saving time

At work, getting clarity around what other people expect is a challenge. People trained in this style of coaching have found it a really useful way of uncovering more information. As a result the job gets done better and faster, saving time and money and leaving people much more motivated.

Tai, a manager in a retail company, describes some benefits he found in using Five-Minute Coach questions with his own line manager: 'On a couple of occasions my boss had asked me to complete a project and write a report and recommendations. Both times he kept asking me to make further changes to the work. However, two months ago, when he gave me another project, I was able to ask him the Five-Minute Coach questions I'd just learned. It was brilliant. I got so much more information about what he wanted. And he found it really helpful to get clear himself on certain things. When he got my report he loved it – first time round!'

Improving team work

We work with teams regularly and too frequently come across teams comprising talented, experienced individuals, who together somehow just don't deliver to expectations. We use the Five-Minute Coach framework to work with a team on defining its goal(s), ensuring a shared understanding, agreeing a team action plan and motivating team members to take action. It's a swift method to coach a team for improved joint performance and better results.

Andy, a learning and development head with a government department, says: 'Following the coaching my team took ownership of the new management training programme, started communicating it and got people interested. Most of the old "silo" mentality has gone and they are working together to make it a success.'

Fostering greater interest in the classroom

Teachers have used the Five-Minute Coach questions in schools in a variety of ways, and are reporting many benefits. The nature of the questions leads pupils to feel better listened to by their teacher, therefore becoming more engaged and focused on lessons.

Geeta, an ICT teacher, says: 'I have been asking these questions recently when behaviour is going awry – either with an individual, group or the whole class. Just asking "What needs to happen for you to stay focused on this lesson?" has been really helpful. I listen to their answers, get more information if I need it, and then I change the way I talk about things to reflect what they have said.'

Maintaining resilience

Staying resilient and avoiding burnout is increasingly difficult in these times of people being asked to deliver more whilst resources are being cut substantially.

Isabella, a community advice centre worker, says: 'I've been seeing more and more people with problems recently. And I'd be giving them advice yet worrying that they don't have what it takes to put it into practice, and we had no more support services to offer due to the cuts. Initially it was a challenge to use only the Five-Minute Coach questions with clients – they tend to feel powerless and want me to tell them what to do. My first taste of the joys of Five-Minute Coach was when I ran through a session, making a mental note to give some information at the end, but found at the finish that the client had her own solution. Now I use the Five-Minute Coach a lot to listen and tease out people's own solutions. I find my job *much* less stressful.'

Improving relationships

People in conflict are often entrenched in their way of thinking and therefore inflexible in their behaviour. The Five-Minute Coach has been used to effect change in relationships with ongoing disagreement, conflict and blame.

Priti, a pastoral manager in a secondary school, reports: 'Many of the problems I deal with are relationship issues between students. They antagonise each other, get over-emotional and are in no state to learn. I've found the Five-Minute Coach questions really useful in getting the youngsters to think differently, first separately, and then together. It helps them to start thinking about what they want rather than staying stuck in the spiral that they're in. It helps them to take responsibility for what happens between them, rather than me telling them what to do. I recently used it with two students who'd been at loggerheads all term. Last week I saw them laughing together on their way to a lesson. Fantastic!'

Generating new leadership styles

Many managers find that having the skills to coach team members quickly and effectively is transforming the way they lead. The old command-and-control approach disappears, as they coach, support and develop their teams.

Wanda, a senior manager, said: 'Since their training in the Five-Minute Coach, all the managers reporting to me are now leading very differently. They are getting people to think for themselves, be reflective and make their own decisions. I have noticed a real change in the atmosphere at work – managers and team members. People are still working hard but are calmer, happier and somehow more respectful of each other. It's a real culture change.'

Reconciling people

One mediator we know has been using the Five-Minute Coach process with clients and has found it enormously helpful in giving people the opportunity to look at what they would like, rather than staying caught up in the current problem.

Jay, a mediator, says: 'I used the Five-Minute Coach to mediate between neighbours. Often in mediation the original cause of conflict has long been forgotten and buried under a continual process of resentment and persistent antagonism. One party presented me with piles of letters and photographs about a tree in his neighbour's garden. He was so caught up in the conflict it was difficult for him to move beyond the dispute. The coaching began with him wanting the tree felled, and ended with him wanting to burn the paperwork and chat with the tree!'

Creating group vision

The Five-Minute Coach has been used by community volunteers to create an inspiring vision of their area, which is currently rated as one of high deprivation.

Marcelina, a community facilitator, reports: 'We used a round-robin format. Everyone took a turn to work out the possible consequences of our vision, and adapt it accordingly. We then answered the action planning questions in turn and developed a plan. Everyone was relaxed because they knew they'd get a turn to contribute. We were really inspired. It's going to take a while to achieve, but we're all really committed to making it happen.'

Clarifying life goals

Although originally used in a work context, the Five-Minute Coach is very helpful in enabling people to explore and make changes in their personal lives too.

Symon, a draughtsman, says: 'I wanted to get clear on what to do with my time and my life, including where to live. As I like the Five-Minute Coach, I asked a colleague who is also trained in the approach to coach me on this very personal and important subject. It removed all the different dialogues I have been having with myself and distracting myself with. Instead, I now have a shape of what I am heading for and I am steadily researching and moving towards what I can do, and when, to change my life.'

Recovering control

The Five-Minute Coach has been used in a number of ways to help people to regain a sense of control over their lives.

Janice, the manager of a women's refuge, reports: 'The women here have endured years of abuse. It seems the effort of getting away from an abuser has taken all their energy, and they struggle to begin to adjust to a normal life. We trained advisors in the Five-Minute Coach and it's proved hugely successful. The whole ethos – the silences that pace the session, the repetition of the woman's words, showing that what she says is important, and giving no advice – has proved invaluable in gently encouraging women to participate and begin to run their own lives.'

Achieving big goals

All forms of coaching can support people to aim for goals that may seem ambitious or even unrealistic. The Five-Minute Coach, with its lack of judgement or interference from the coach, helps people explore their dreams thoroughly, often with dramatic results.

Danica, a therapist, reports: 'I'd been thinking about setting up a fire walk for ages, but didn't think it was possible. During coaching my fears all came out. What would it entail? How challenging could it be to get permission from the council? And so on. As part of my action plan I realised the first thing I needed to do was make the call to the council. I did it, got a "maybe" and stayed motivated to keep on going. They set me lots of hurdles, which I may have fallen at before. But I did everything. I got a positive result – the public fire walk was hugely successful. Coaching really helped me to achieve what I'd thought was impossible.'

Designing and planning

Several people have told us how they find the Five-Minute Coach useful in planning, structuring and mapping out different kinds of projects.

Jono, an art director, loves to use the Five-Minute Coach approach to help him create and plan the books he designs. He says: 'I ask myself the questions when I want to structure a flat plan for books and for other projects too. For me the Five-Minute Coach is like a flow chart, a kind of mathematics. It helps me bridge the creativity and the need for planning and structure.'

Creating new concepts

People have used the Five-Minute Coach in developing creative concepts, either themselves or with others. They find the questions, with the lack of comment or judgement, stimulate new ideas, connections and concepts.

Shona, a writer of recipe books, says: 'As well as using the Five-Minute Coach to work with others, I love asking the question of myself when I want to create dishes. When I'm at the market, I might say to myself, "The lamb looks fantastic!" Then I find that I'm asking myself: "And then what happens?" Ideas of dishes then spring to mind. I ask myself more questions about the dish (such as "What kind of ...?", "Is there anything else about the dish?"). It's a very good way of thinking things through and I've developed some creative and successful dishes.'

Parenting

Youngsters, particularly teens, often complain about not being listened to or understood by their parents (and of course the opposite is true too!). Communications between the generations can be eased by parents carefully using their children's words, as well as some well-placed Five-Minute Coach questions.

Liz, a mother of two, says: 'When I started to use Five-Minute Coach questions with my 15-year-old daughter I started to get much more information. Simple things like "What kind of gig?" seemed to start a more productive dialogue than "Will there be alcohol?" as my opening gambit, or worse, "You're not old enough." It keeps things calmer, takes the judgement out of my voice and helps us to explore rather than battle.'

Moving beyond inherited stereotypes

The Five-Minute Coach offers a non-confrontational way of changing expectations. It's been used in a number of contexts. One such example comes from youth work, in a situation where groups of young people had unhelpful perceptions of each other and there was little communication.

Cliff, a youth leader, reported: 'We've had a problem integrating locals and incomers to the area. So I asked one local lad what he'd like to have happen. He told me he wanted a group of youngsters to go away – although he put it in more colourful terms! Rather than challenge what was probably something he'd heard at home, I just asked, "And then what happens?" After a few repetitions, he said, "OK, I get it! I'd end up being alone. And I don't want that!" With one simple question he'd changed his mind. Faster, easier and, to be honest, more successful than my usual attempts at convincing these youngsters to think differently.'

Returning power to people

People who have a tendency to take responsibility for making everything right for someone else have been liberated from some of that burden by the Five-Minute Coach. They use the questions to give decisions and choices back to the owner of a problem, in a way that is constructive and feels positive.

Meena, a care home manager, explained: 'I often get residents coming into my office saying "I feel bad because ..." They want me to make things better. Now I've discovered a question to make them stop and think. I ask "And what would you like to have happen?" It's changed the whole conversation. They start to realise that despite being cared for by me and my staff, they aren't dependent on us for everything. It's amazing how it puts power back into their hands. And, if it's an issue about our service, they sometimes give me some great ideas.'

Better appraisals

Although appraisals and performance reviews are a necessity of the job, many managers dislike doing them, fearing what they'll hear or what they need to challenge.

Alex, a manager, says: 'Since learning the Five-Minute Coach, I use a couple of questions regularly. The most useful one, during appraisals, is "What kind of ...?" when staff describe a situation or how something makes them feel. One member of staff said she was resentful about something. Asking "What kind of resentful?" really opened up the conversation, gave her the chance to think more deeply and helped to pinpoint the issue. I got more information and she felt more heard.'

Selling more

Good sales can be hard to achieve for businesses in any sector. We've heard from a number people who have used Five-Minute Coach questions to improve their conversations with customers and boost their sales.

Sasha, a shopkeeper, was delighted to report: 'When shoppers come in, I engage them in conversation and always ask "What kind of ...?" if they tell me they're looking for something in particular. Whether I have it or not, I conclude with "And is there anything else you'd like?" and – I'm happy to say – there usually is!'

Chapter 12

Developing as a Coach

One of the challenges faced by people coaching others within the same organisation – whether they be direct reports, colleagues or even bosses – is keeping clear boundaries between the different 'hats' they wear. Not so when coaching with the Five-Minute Coach. It restricts your ability to provide any input to the person you're working with, unlike when you're working as a mentor, manager, consultant, trainer, advisor or counsellor.

If you put into practice what you learn from this book you will have very quickly adopted the following principles of good coaching:

● Coaching helps people learn from the inside out, not the other way around.[11] It assumes that people have innate capabilities and therefore do not need to be constantly told *what* to do.

● Focusing on outcomes – what could be, rather than what is – is fundamental to the unleashing of people's potential and upgrading their performance.

● Coaching encourages individuals, through support and increased self-awareness, to take personal responsibility for creating their own opportunities, making their own choices and deciding on their own actions.

● An individual's self-belief grows through the coaching process, and new thinking, feelings and behaviours emerge as a result.

The Five-Minute Coach is built on these principles. If you are new to coaching, then learning to coach this way will accelerate your own skill development and understanding of the core of coaching – something that many trainee coaches take much longer to discover and integrate.

If you are actively using, or still experimenting with, the Five-Minute Coach, you may want to take one of two paths. You could deepen your skills in this type of coaching to integrate into your

---

11 Bluckert, P. (2006). *Psychological Dimensions of Executive Coaching.* McGraw Hill Education.

management and communications style, or you could expand your skills and knowledge to actively become a coach.

Should you be content to assimilate this coaching into your day-to-day work, using it as a tool to engage and support others, we'd recommend you keep practising and building your skills further. In Chapter 13 you'll find a guide to a range of resources including books and training.

If, however, you've found using the Five-Minute Coach so rewarding that you are now keen to make coaching a larger part of your work portfolio, you have a variety of options. Many organisations have in-house coaches who are trained to work throughout the business supporting employees where required. A number of voluntary organisations use coaches to support members of a diverse range of community groups. There is also now a substantial market for independent coaches working with organisations or individuals to offer a range of services such as executive coaching, leadership coaching, career coaching and life coaching.

Coaching professionally

To pursue coaching at a more professional level, there are a number of areas where you can both develop and receive support as you grow as a coach. The four key areas are: coach training, membership of professional bodies, accreditation, and coaching supervision and continuous professional development (CPD).

Coach training

Firstly, you may want to enrich your understanding of the Five-Minute Coach or learn more generally about coaching cleanly. You'll find how to access such training opportunities in Chapter 13.

Secondly, to learn alternative coaching techniques – and a range of other essential skills for the professional coach (such as contracting, evaluation, ethical issue management, relationship management and more) – you can go online for information on coach training courses. For guidance, the professional coaching bodies (see below) accredit or endorse certain coach training programmes, so you may wish to research courses through their websites.

Membership of professional bodies

Listed below are a number of professional coaching associations in the UK and Europe, and some have a global presence too. You'll find out more about their membership criteria, support and services on their websites. Further coaching bodies also exist internationally and can be found through an internet search.

Association for Coaching (AC)
www.associationforcoaching.com

Association for Professional Executive Coaching and Supervision (APECS)
www.apecs.org

BACP Coaching (a division of the British Association for Counselling and Psychotherapy)
www.bacpcoaching.co.uk

European Mentoring and Coaching Council (EMCC)
www.emccouncil.org

International Coach Federation (ICF)
www.coachfederation.org

Coaching is currently a self-regulated profession, and the aims of the professional bodies include promoting best practice and improving standards. Membership of a coaching body provides the coach with support, a range of development opportunities and a set of ethical guidelines. (The Association for Coaching's Code of Ethics can be found in Appendix III.) In addition, many offer accreditation for coaches.

Accreditation

A range of coach accreditation schemes exist. Accreditation requires certain levels of training, experience, coaching supervision and other ongoing learning and development. Accreditation offers coaches a path of professional development and recognition of skills and achievements. For coachees and purchasers of coaching services, a coach's accredited status offers a level of quality assurance.

Accreditation is available through the professional bodies – visit their websites for more information.

Coaching supervision and continuous professional development

If you are serious about coaching you'll also be serious about your own development as a coach. In the drive to increase standards across the profession, coaching supervision is increasingly used to support coaching practice. Coaching supervisors can be found through the Association of Coaching Supervisors (www.association ofcoachingsupervisors.com) or through professional coaching bodies.

Professional coaches also undertake CPD to extend and embed their skills. A myriad of opportunities for learning are available, from books and articles to seminars and coaching conferences.

Whether you choose to use the Five-Minute Coach to improve performance at work, as a starting point for a coaching career or to add to the tools and techniques you already use as a professional coach, you'll find the quality of your conversations transformed.

Chapter 13
Exploring Further Resources

Now that you have discovered the Five-Minute Coach, your journey may just be beginning. If you are curious to learn more about this kind of coaching, its roots or to develop your skills in using this approach, there are plenty of options to do more.

Learning more about the Five-Minute Coach

You'll find a range of ideas for pursuing your understanding and knowledge of the Five-Minute Coach below. More information about each can be found on www.thefive-minutecoach.co.uk.

Experiencing the Five-Minute Coach

Many people find that, once they have started using the Five-Minute Coach, they want to hone their skills in a structured and supportive environment. Like them, you may find it useful to attend one of the training events that run regularly.

Organisational training

If you want your organisation to benefit, then bespoke in-house training programmes complete with coaching supervision and CPD for Five-Minute Coaches, are available.

Observing the Five-Minute Coach

Now that you've read the book, you may want to round off your experience by seeing or hearing the Five Minute Coach in action. Access some short video clips, plus downloadable MP3 audio files for each stage of the Five-Minute Coach, via the web site. This will give you an idea of the pace, cadence of questions and other nuances.

Accessing other resources

If you're a member of LinkedIn join the Five-Minute Coach Group to share experiences and questions with other members, and refer to the Five-Minute Coach web site for updates on further ways in which to access information via social media.

Using other languages

The framework is available in a number of languages in addition to English. Please visit the web site for more information.

Learning more about Clean Language

The Five-Minute Coach has been created using the principles and approach of Clean Language and Symbolic Modelling. To find out much more about these visit www.cleanlanguage.co.uk . Here you'll find an extensive range of articles, access to the Clean Forum and an array of other resources. Further opportunities for learning about Clean language are outlined below.

Attending events

For a good introduction to where and how Clean Language is used, and to obtain some practical experience, you can attend a Clean Conference. Information can be found at www.cleanconference. co.uk.

You'll discover organisations that provide training in clean techniques on www.cleanlanguage.co.uk.

Practising your skills

As a way of learning more clean questions and practising your clean questioning skills, you may wish to experiment with the Clean Change Cards, available at www.anglo-american.co.uk, which in addition stocks the books we mention below.

Reading more about Clean Language

If you are keen to read a practical book that develops your use of clean questions when working with metaphor, then this step-by-step guide fits the bill: *Clean Language: Revealing Metaphors and Opening Minds* by Wendy Sullivan and Judy Rees (Crown House Publishing, 2008).

If you would like to know more, then one book that is a must-read, covers Clean Language, Symbolic Modelling, the theory of metaphor, self-organising systems and the therapeutic process: *Metaphors in Mind: Transformation through Symbolic Modelling* by James Lawley and Penny Tompkins (Developing Company Press, 2000).

The Five-Minute Coach Framework

Stage	Purpose	Questions
1	Identifying an outcome	**And what would you like to have happen?**
2	Choosing the best outcome	**And when** [outcome in coachee's words], **_then_ what happens?** **And when** [last answer], **_then_ what happens?** (Repeat question, with each answer, until no new answers emerge) **And** [outcome] **and** [recap all answers], **what are you drawn to most?**
3	Discovering more about the outcome	**And when** [new outcome], **what kind of** [word or phrase from outcome]**?** **And when** [last answer], **is there anything else about** [same word or phrase]**?** **And when** [last answer], **where is/are** [same word or phrase]**?** **And when** [last answer], **whereabouts** [last answer]**?** **And** [last answer]. **Given what you _now_ know, what would you like to have happen?**
4	Action planning	**And what needs to happen for** [final outcome]**?** **And is there anything else that needs to happen for** [final outcome]**?** (Repeat question until you hear first 'no') **And** [final outcome and recap every action point], **and is there anything else that needs to happen for** [final outcome]**?** (Repeat question until you hear second 'no') **And** [final outcome and recap every action point], **and what needs to happen _first_?** **And can** [previous answer]**?**
5	Motivate to act	**And when** [first thing], **_then_ what happens?** (Repeat until coachee is in a positive state and seems keen to act) **And is that a good place to stop?** (Hand over notes)

Remember:

1 Pay close attention
2 Use only the Five-Minute Coach questions
3 Avoid the normal rules of conversation
4 Repeat the coachee's words
5 Disregard grammatical rules

6 Take notes
7 Limit eye contact
8 Encourage the coachee
9 Use voice to influence
10 Stay cool, calm and collected

Appendix II:
Full Five-Minute Coach Example Transcript – Amira and Chris

Through Chapters 2–7 you will have read parts of an example Five-Minute Coach session transcript which was relevant to the stage of the framework you were learning. Here is the entire transcript, followed by the coach's handwritten notes in full.

Amira:	And where would you like to sit (gesturing around the space)?
Chris:	(Sits down)
Amira:	And where would you like me to sit?
Chris:	Hmm – over there? (Chris points and Amira sits down)
Amira:	Let me explain a little about this coaching. My job is to help you to explore your issue, work out what you want and how you are going to achieve it. I won't be offering you ideas or suggestions as to how to do it.
	You'll soon find that this isn't like a normal conversation or even any coaching session you may have had before. I won't look at you much, and I won't make any suggestions or comments about what you say.
	I will be taking notes to help me remember what you've said. And at the end, I'll give you all the notes.
	Anything you say is confidential, unless it's illegal or unsafe.
	If I ask you any questions that seem unusual or odd, just answer with the first thing that comes to mind.
	Once we start, I won't answer any questions as that will interrupt the flow. So … is there anything you'd like to ask me now?

Chris: This definitely sounds like something new! OK, I'll give it a try.

Amira: **And what would you like to have happen?**

Chris: Now that Jane's gone, and I'm not allowed to replace her, I'd like to know what work I can just *not* do.

Amira: **And when** you know what work you can just *not* do, ***then* what happens?**

Chris: Then half my to-do list vanishes and only the important things are left.

Amira: **And when** only the important things are left, ***then* what happens?**

Chris: Then I stay focused, I can go through things easily to work out the priorities, make the connections, skim the folder of non-priority stuff looking only for things that relate to the priorities I'm tackling.

Amira: **And when** you stay focused, work out priorities, make connections, skim the folder looking only for things that relate to priorities, ***then* what happens?**

Chris: Then I meet my deadlines.

Amira: **And when** you meet your deadlines, ***then* what happens?**

Chris: Then people will come to me for my experience, I won't let them down.

Amira: **And when** people come to you and you won't let them down, ***then* what happens?**

Chris: I'll get involved in the more challenging projects and get a good reputation ... and maybe I won't get overlooked when the next departmental manager job comes up.

Amira: **And when** you're involved in more challenging projects, get a good reputation and maybe won't get overlooked when the next manager job comes up, ***then* what happens?**

Chris: Then I do a better job, enjoy it more and I'm on track to move up the career ladder – and earn more!

Amira: **And when** you do a better job, move up the career ladder and earn more**, *then* what happens?**

Chris: Then I'm very happy!

Amira: **And when** you're very happy, *then* **what happens?**

Chris: I should have said I'm very happy *and* successful!

Amira: **And when** you're happy *and* successful, *then* **what happens?**

Chris: Hmm ... nothing else!

Amira: **And** you'd like to know what work you can just not do. **And** half your to-do list vanishes and only the important things are left ... you stay focused, you go through things easily to work out the priorities, make the connections, skim the folder of non-priority stuff looking only for things that relate to the priorities you're tackling ... you meet your deadlines ... people come to you for your experience, you won't let them down ... you get more involved in the more challenging projects and get a good reputation and maybe won't get overlooked when the next departmental manager job comes up ... you do a better job, move up the career ladder and earn more ... and you're very happy. **What are you drawn to most?**

Chris: Focusing, prioritising and meeting important deadlines.

Amira: **And when** focusing, prioritising and meeting important deadlines, **what kind of** prioritising?

Chris: Standing back, and creating space to think.

Amira: **And when** standing back and creating space to think, **is there anything else about** prioritising?

Chris: Yes. It's about what's important, what's urgent. Actually what bits of work will make a difference.

Amira: **And when** it's about what's important, what's urgent, what bits of work will make a difference, **where is** prioritising**?**

Chris: I'm not sure ... actually it's in front of me.

Amira: **And when** it's in front of you, **whereabouts** in front of you**?**

Chris: Just here (Chris gestures to a space from left to right of his body, at waist level).

Amira: **And it's there** (pointing to space Chris has just indicated). **Given what you *now* know, what would you like to have happen?**

Chris: I'd like to find it easy to meet my deadlines.

Amira: **And what needs to happen for** you to find it easy to meet your deadlines**?**

Chris: I need to set time aside to go through all the information on my desk and computer so that I can determine my priorities.

Amira: **And is there anything *else* that needs to happen for** you to find it easy to meet your deadlines**?**

Chris: I need to look at what's urgent, and what's important.

Amira: **And is there anything *else* that needs to happen for** you to find it easy to meet your deadlines**?**

Chris: I need to check in with you as to what you think is most important.

Amira: **And is there anything *else* that needs to happen for** you to find it easy to meet your deadlines**?**

Chris: I need to show you my list of priorities and make sure it's agreed.

Amira: **And is there anything *else* that needs to happen for** you to find it easy to meet your deadlines**?**

Chris: I need to get rid of some things ... pass other things on to Alex.

Amira:	**And is there anything *else* that needs to happen for** you to find it easy to meet your deadlines?

Chris: No.

Amira: **And** to find it easy to meet your deadlines, you need to set time aside to go through all the information on your desk and computer so that you can determine your priorities ... look at what's urgent and what's important ... check in with me as to what I think is important ... show me your list of priorities and make sure it's agreed ... get rid of some things, pass other things on to Alex. **And is there anything *else* that needs to happen for** you to find it easy to meet your deadlines?

Chris: I need to make sure that I know which pieces of work will make most impact, you know, make a difference.

Amira: **And is there anything *else* that needs to happen for** you to find it easy to meet your deadlines?

Chris: I need to block some time out in my diary for each of my priorities.

Amira: **And is there anything *else* that needs to happen for** you to find it easy to meet your deadlines?

Chris: I need to set some mini targets – stepping stones – to ensure that each deadline is on target for being met.

Amira: **And is there anything *else* that needs to happen for** you to find it easy to meet all your deadlines?

Chris: No.

Amira: **And** to find it easy to meet all your deadlines, you need to set time aside to go through all the information on your desk and computer so that you can determine your priorities ... look at what's urgent and what's important ... check in with me as to what I think is important ... show me your list of priorities and make sure it's agreed ... get rid of some things, pass other things on to Alex ... make sure you know which pieces of work will make a difference ... block some time out in your diary for each of your priorities ... set some mini targets – stepping stones – to ensure that each deadline is on target for being met. **And what needs to happen first?**

Chris: I need to set time aside and go through the information on my desk and computer, so I can begin to prioritise.

Amira: **And can** you set time aside and go through the information on your desk and computer, and begin to prioritise**?**

Chris: Yes!

Amira: **And when** you set time aside and go through the information on your desk and computer, and begin to prioritise, *then* **what happens?**

Chris: Then I can check in with you and agree the priorities.

Amira: **And when** you check in with me and agree the priorities, *then* **what happens?**

Chris: Then I block time in my diary to tackle each piece of work.

Amira: **And when** you block time in your diary to tackle each piece of work, *then* **what happens?**

Chris: Then I achieve the deadlines.

Amira: Hmm (nodding). **And when** you *achieve* the deadlines, *then* **what happens?**

Chris: Then I feel great – and others will notice I'm on top of things too.

Amira: **And when** you feel *great* – and (next words said slowly) others will notice you're on top of things too, *then* **what happens?**

Chris: Then I'll be better placed to move up to a bigger job (big smile on face).

Amira: **And** (big smile on face too) **is that a good place to stop?**

Chris: Yes!

Amira: (Hands over notes) Thank you. And if you'd like to let me
          know how you get on, then please do.

	Chris Coaching 25 October
WLH	Now Jane's gone + I'm X allowd 2 replace, like to know what wk can just not do
—	
WLH	1/2 my To Do list vamishes + only imp things R left
TWH	Stay focused, can go thru' things easily 2 wk out priorities, make connections, skim x-priority stuff, lookg only 4 things relate 2 priorities
TWH	Mt my deadlines
TWH	Pple come 2 me. I won't let them down
TWH	Involved in > challenging projs, get gd reputn + maybe X get overlkd when next mgr's job comes up
TWH	Do bttr job, enjoy >, move ↑ career ladder, earn >
TWH	V. happy
TWH	V. happy + successful
TWH	—
DTM	Focusg, prioritising + mtg imp deadlines
—	
WKO	Standg back + creatg space 2 think
AE	What's imp, what's urgent, what bits wk will make diff
W	In front of me
WA	Just here
Now WLH	2 find it easy 2 mt my deadlines

WNH	Set time aside 2 go thru all info on desk on + computer so can determine priorities
AE	Look at what's urgent + what's imp
AE	Check in with u, what think's most imp.
AE	Show u my list priorities + make sure agreed
AE	Get rid some things, pass others → Alex
AE	No
AE	Make sure know which pieces wk will make most impact/difference
AE	Block some time out, in diary, 4 each of priorities
AE	Set some mini-tgts, steppg stones 2 ensure each ddline on tgt4 being met
AE	—
1st	Set time aside + go thru info on desk + compr so can begin 2 prioritise
Can	Yes
—	
TWH	Check in with u + agree priorities
TWH	Block time in diary to tackle each pce wk
TWH	Achieve deadlines
TWH	Feel great. Others know I'm on top of things
TWH	Better placed to ↑ to bigger job
Stop	Yes

Appendix III:

Association for Coaching's Code of Ethics and Good Coaching Practice

The Association for Coaching (AC) is committed to maintaining excellent coaching practice. This Code of Ethics and Good Coaching Practice sets out the essential elements of sound ethical practice. For the purposes of this code, the person receiving coaching is called the Client.

All Clients should expect a high standard of practice from their Coach. To ensure that this is achieved Coaches commit to operate in accordance with the Association's Code of Ethics and Good Coaching Practice for ethical, competent and effective practice.

1   Coaches are required to recognise both personal and professional limitations:

Personal – with respect to maintaining their own good health and fitness to practice. Should this not be the case, Coaches are required to withdraw from their practice until such time as they are in good health and fit to resume. Clients should be offered appropriate, alternative support during any such period.

Professional – with respect to whether their experience is appropriate to meet the Client's requirements. When this is not the case, Clients should be referred to other appropriate services, e.g. more experienced Coaches, Counsellors, Psychotherapists or other specialist services. In particular, Coaches are required to be sensitive to the possibility that some Clients will require more psychological support than is normally available within the coaching remit. In these cases, referral should be made to an appropriate source of care, e.g. the Client's GP, a Counsellor or Psychotherapist, psychological support services and/or agencies.

© Association for Coaching

2   Coaches are responsible for ensuring that Clients are fully informed of the coaching contract and terms and conditions for coaching both prior to and at the initial session. These matters include confidentiality, sessional costs and frequency of sessions. All claims made by the Coach should be honest, accurate and consistent with maintaining the coaching profession's good standing. All coaching contracts should make clear that in the case of any illegal activity becoming evident during the coaching, or if there is potential for harm to be caused to the Client or others, the Coach may not be able to maintain complete Client confidentiality and may need to involve others. Where possible and appropriate, the Coach will do this with the permission and consensus of the Client. In the case of coaching children, specific agreement should be reached with the sponsors and the child regarding the level of confidentiality to ensure the wellbeing of the child.

3   Coaches are required to be frank and willing to respond to their Client's requests for information about the methods, techniques and ways in which the coaching process will be conducted. This should be done both prior to contract agreement and during the full term of the contract.

4   Coaches must be sensitive to issues of culture, religion, gender, sexuality, disability and race and all other forms of equalities and diversity.

5   Coaches must respect the Client's right to terminate coaching at any point during the coaching process.

6   Coaches are required to maintain appropriate records of their work with Clients, ensuring that any such records are accurate and that reasonable security precautions are taken to protect against third party disclosure. Attention must be given to the Coachee's rights under any current legislation, such as the Data Protection Act.

7   Coaches are required to monitor the quality of their work and to seek feedback wherever possible from Clients and other professionals as appropriate.

© Association for Coaching

8 Coaches are expected to have regular consultative support for their work, typically in the form of an appropriately qualified and experienced coaching supervisor. Further details on coaching supervision can be found on the AC website.

9 A Coach should aim to undertake a minimum of 30 hours of continuing professional development (CPD) in the theory and practice of coaching on an annual basis, which is required for both continued AC membership and individual Coach accreditation.

10 Coaches are required to keep themselves informed of any statutory or legal requirements that may affect their work and comply fully with them.

11 Coaches are required to have current professional liability insurance that specifically includes coaching as a work activity.

12 Coaches are required to consider the impact of any dual relationships they may hold with regards to their Clients and/ or any sponsoring organisations. If such a relationship is identified, then it must be made clear to all parties involved so that agreement may be reached about whether to continue the coaching relationship.

13 Any Coach working with children must have a relevant Criminal Records Bureau (CRB) check before commencing coaching.

14 Coaches must act in a manner that does not bring the profession of coaching into disrepute.

© Association for Coaching

References

Bluckert, P. (2006). *Psychological Dimensions of Executive Coaching.* McGraw Hill Education.

Cooper, L. (2008). *Business NLP for Dummies.* John Wiley & Sons.

Grove, D. (1998). The Philosophy and Principles of Clean Language. Available at www.cleanlanguage.co.uk/articles/articles/38/1/ (accessed 6 January 2012).

Kline, N. (1999). *Time to Think: Listening to Ignite the Human Mind.* Cassell Illustrated.

Lawley, J. and Tompkins, P. (2000). *Metaphors in Mind: Transformation through Symbolic Modelling.* Developing Company Press.

Lawley, J. and Tompkins, P. (2012). A Framework for Change. Available at www.cleanlanguage.co.uk/articles/articles/313/1/ (accessed 6 January 2012).

O'Neill, M. (2000). *Executive Coaching with Backbone and Heart: A Systems Approach to Engaging Leaders with Their Challenges.* Jossey-Bass.

Sullivan, W. and Rees, J. (2008). *Clean Language: Revealing Metaphors and Opening Minds.* Crown House Publishing.

Tompkins, P. and Lawley, J. (2000). Coaching for P.R.O.'s. Available at www.cleanlanguage.co.uk/articles/articles/31/ (accessed 6 January 2012).

Tompkins, P. and Lawley, J. (2004). When and How to Use 'When' and 'As'. Available at www.cleanlanguage.co.uk/articles/articles/212/1/ (accessed 6 January 2012).

Index